THE CHURCHYARDS HANDBOOK

ADVICE ON THEIR CARE AND MAINTENANCE

SECOND EDITION

Revised for the Council for Places of Worship

by

THE REV. HENRY STAPLETON, FSA

and

PETER BURMAN, FSA

D1394207

CIO PUBLISHING

Church House, Dean's Yard,
London SW1P 3NZ
1976

THE EDITORS

The Rev. Henry Stapleton is a member of the Council for Places of Worship and of the Norwich Diocesan Advisory Committee; formerly (for 13 years) Secretary of the York Diocesan Advisory Committee.

Peter Busman is the Deputy Secretary of the Council for Places of Worship and Cathedrals Advisory Committee.

Published for the Council for Places of Worship
© The Central Board of Finance of the Church of England, 1976

ISBN 0 7151 7529 7

First edition 1962
Second edition 1976

PRINTED IN GREAT BRITAIN BY HEADLEY BROTHERS LTD
109 KINGSWAY LONDON WC2B 6PX AND ASHFORD KENT

Contents

APPENDICES

List of illustrations

Acknowledgements

The Editors have received a great deal of help and encouragement from others and wish especially to thank the following:

Dr P. V. Addyman; Mr Andrew Anderson; Sir John Betjeman, Poet Laureate, and SPCK (publishers) for permission to reproduce in the opening chapter lines from one of his *Poems in the Porch*; Mr Ian Bristow; Mr Hugh Brogan; Mrs Pamela Burgess; The Rev. Dr Gilbert Cope; Mr Felix Crowder; Mr J. H. Davies of the Agricultural Development and Advisory Service; Mr F. G. Dimes of the Geological Museum; The Rev. the Worshipful Chancellor K. J. T. Elphinstone; The Worshipful Company of Gardeners; The Worshipful Chancellor Bradley Goodman; The Rev. the Worshipful Chancellor E. Garth Moore; Mr Gunnar Godwin; Mr Eric Hoare of the Joint Committee for the British Monumental Industry; The Legal Advisory Commission of the General Synod of the Church of England and its Secretary, Mr Brian Hanson; Mr Kenneth Lindley; The Rev. Kenneth Loveless; The Rev. O. Muspratt, Rector of Penn, Bucks; The Rev. P. N. Pare; Chancellor Arthur Phillips, OBE; Mr Darsie Rawlins; Mr John Robinson of the Church Commissioners; the County Planning Officer for Staffordshire; Mr Laurence Whistler, CBE; Dr H. Leslie White; Miss Corinne Wilson; Mr David Williams, Mrs I. E. Young and Mrs M. L. Cleave, of the Council's staff; and Mrs Jean Bygrave who typed the final text.

1. *Churchyards—an explanation and a manifesto*

It is over forty years since the publication of the first edition of the *Care of Churchyards* pamphlet. The influence of that book and its successor, the *Churchyards Handbook* of 1962, can be discerned in most English parish churchyards. The general standard of maintenance is higher; the design of gravestones has improved; materials which are inappropriate in an English churchyard are less in evidence. It may be objected that much of what follows is too exclusively concerned with the character of a *country* churchyard. This conceded, it must be acknowledged that churchyards in other settings—e.g. in the centre of a modern industrial city, or in a suburb—require a slightly different emphasis in order to enable them to respond to their own *genius loci*.

We believe, however, that it is time to re-assert the intrinsic character of the churchyard and to define what essentially it is. Many schemes 'for improvement' fail to appreciate the subtlety of its constituents with the result that untold damage is done. We suggest that a churchyard may be defined as 'the area around a church where the dead are buried'.

Scenically the churchyard is part of the religious landscape; not only is it the setting for the church, but theologically it has the significance so well expressed by Bishop Healey in his address to the Royal Society of Arts in 1967: 'Each is incomplete without the other. They are sacramentals; outward and visible forms of the ministering of God's grace to the whole man, who is born, lives and dies, after the order of his creation: and after the order of Redemption is born again, lives and dies to live in Christ. This life is incomplete without death; and the visible church building is incomplete in its witness to this world without this outreach to the dead.'

The churchyard belongs to the community. The present generation is judged by the way it cares for the resting place of its departed members. Grass is the usual covering of the ground. Economic considerations will no doubt diminish the enthusiasm of those who would have the whole area a lawn and there is a commendable return to the ancient method of keeping the grass tidy by grazing. The gravestones are not obstacles preventing the speedy manœuvre of the lawnmower;

they are the markers indicating the burial of a body beneath, they are the stone books recording the history of the parish. Ecologically there are many churchyards which are natural conservation areas. The subtlety of these constituents means that great sensitivity is needed to maintain a balance between the complete chaos on the one hand and obsessive tidiness on the other. But these positive principles carry corresponding negations.

First, the churchyard is not the same as an area around a house; it is not solely a garden. It is the area round a *church*. There is no need for flowers, flower beds for annuals or herbaceous borders. How many of these are generously donated and cared for for a short period of time and then neglected! Rarely does enthusiasm last until the time when the roses grow old and need replacement; herbaceous plants must be all dug up and split annually. Again, too many small shrubs or flowering cherries can soon transform a churchyard into the resemblance of a suburban garden. The time-honoured name is 'God's Acre' which presents the sturdy image of a good agricultural field with solid forest trees on the boundary. Our present Poet Laureate, Sir John Betjeman, has expressed all that is intended here in succinct and memorable words:

> I hate to see in old churchyards
> Tombstones stacked round like playing cards
> Along the wall which then encloses
> A trim new lawn and standard roses,
> Bird-baths and objects such as fill a
> Garden in some suburban villa.
> The Bishop comes; the bird-bath's blessed,
> Our churchyard's now a 'garden of rest'.
> And so it may be; all the the same
> Graveyard's a much more honest name.
>
> (*Poems in the Porch*, SPCK, 1954)

Perhaps the most powerful pressure on churchyards has been from those who would have this area neat and tidy (*see* Fig 1). Many look askance at the churchyard and criticise its long grass and unkempt appearance. There are some villages where not a single blade of grass at roadside or in garden may grow more than an inch! The cult of the lawn can lead its devotees to the point where all gravestones have to be sacrificed in honour of the omnivorous mower. To keep the churchyard like a lawn is expensive in equipment and labour even if help is obtained from the local authority. While we grant that in certain built-up areas there may be a case for the close cutting of grass we repeat our contention that the intrinsic character of a churchyard as 'the area round a church where the dead are buried' should be preserved. However, a compromise is needed between an excuse for complete neglect and obsessive tidiness and we commend the simple expedient of cutting the grass short beside paths and leaving the rest for occasional cutting. This treatment keeps the proper character of the churchyard at minimal expense.

Secondly, a churchyard is not solely a setting for an ancient monument. At the centre of a churchyard stands not a ruin or a museum but a church, a place of worship for some week by week, for others who attend less frequently the house of God for baptisms, weddings and funerals. Much as one may admire the smooth lawns around an ancient abbey or castle whose grounds are kept up by the Department of the Environment, there is no necessity for the churchyard sward to be so closely clipped. To maintain such a high standard costs money and most parishes cannot, indeed ought not, to expend large sums in this way. A fee is paid for entry to most ancient monuments; there is no such fee for a parish church.

Thirdly, a churchyard is not simply a place where the dead are buried. For that could be a definition of any burial ground or public cemetery. While it is true that many cemeteries have a chapel or building as a central feature these have relevance only to the *dead*. A church as we have already stated is concerned also with the living. There is the geographical aspect too. A cemetery may serve a very wide area. Many are vast in scale. The churchyard on the other hand is the burial ground of a particular group of people—its parish. It is often possible to find groups of gravestones commemorating several generations of the same family. As an old law case has it, churchyards are where parishioners 'became entitled by law . . . to render back their remains into the earth, the common mother of mankind, without payment for the ground which they were to occupy'. Whereas in a public cemetery there was little attempt until the introduction of 'lawn cemeteries' to promote any congruity with adjacent headstones, in the churchyard a self-discipline of restraint has been exercised over the years to create some harmony of effect. While public cemeteries date for the most part from the nineteenth century, many a churchyard contains burials from the foundation of the church in the Middle Ages or earlier. Again, under recent legislation permission for a memorial

3

stone to stand in a cemetery is given only for a specified number of years; in a churchyard there is no such period defined.

An integral part of the churchyard's character is the gravestones. They are not to be removed to stand around the wall where they are separated from the remains whose position they record. These stones tell the history of a parish perhaps for 300 years or more; they reflect what people feel about death and bereavement; and what craftsmen feel about design and expression—and how taste in these matters constantly changes. The inscriptions not only record names but details of relationships and occupations recorded nowhere else. There are the simple late seventeenth- or early eighteenth-century stones of local material and craftsmanship (see Fig 2); those of the neo-classical elegance (see Fig 3); then the Victorian ones which reveal a great variety in the letter-cutter's art.

Archaeologists, too, are beginning to turn their attention to a study of the development of the churchyard. It is well known that the north side was considered in medieval times as the place for burial of the suicide and unbaptised and this accounts for the absence of stones in this area; in fact many churches were originally built up against a northern boundary. There has, however, not yet been much research into the topology of the churchyard and its development over the centuries. And in any case a churchyard is more than just an archaeological site.

The churchyard and its stones are part of the English scene. The stones provide the scale by which to measure the church. Remove them and, if there are no trees, there may be nothing to which the church can be visually related. It is not without good reason that the photographer of a landscape includes some object in the foreground, a person or a tree for example, to provide this picture with the necessary scale. In this he follows the engraver.

The past two centuries have seen considerable changes in agricultural technique. Of all the grassland in the parish the churchyard's sward alone may have survived undisturbed, untouched perhaps for hundreds of years. With so many pasturelands and parklands being ploughed and treated with herbicide and grass regulants, churchyards often contain the only surviving remnants of ancient grassland (see Fig 4). Here grow wild flowers in profusion: and they should be encouraged to grow. The wildness of a country churchyard can sometimes be peculiarly apt, and the stable environment is a positive encouragement to a rich mixture of flora and fauna. In a Suffolk churchyard recently the County Naturalists' Trust was able to identify more than 300 different varieties of wild flowers and flowering grasses, including a rarely found orchid. As Gerard Manley Hopkins wrote in *Invershaid*:

> What would the world be, once bereft
> Of wet and wildness? Let them be left,
> O let them be left, wildness and wet
> Long live the weeds and the wilderness yet.

Some churchyards, in Norfolk and Suffolk for example, are the only places where the wild orchid can be found; others shelter rare grasses and wild flowers. Long grass is the habitat of the vole and other small animals who in turn provide the food for hawks and kestrels. The trees, alive and dead, provide nesting places for birds and the source of their food supply. The hedges are often the only ones that remain in the district and perform a similar function. Even the lichen is of interest to the naturalist. Each dated stone provides the birthday of the lichen colony.

Amongst the factors affecting the country churchyard in recent years has been the considerable decrease in the number of burials. Cremations now account for over 59 per cent. The Church has endeavoured to demonstrate its concern for the departed by allocating areas for cremated remains; but these have by no means been used as much as was hoped. It is perhaps doubtful whether the percentage of cremations will increase. Many country people prefer the traditional method of earth burial and others like to have the opportunity of erecting a suitable memorial over the place where the dead are interred so that they can pay their respects. This instinctive desire has never really been satisfied by the Book of Remembrance, however beautiful this may be, and other attempts at 'memorialisation' have not yet had much success.

Economics have forced many small country monumental stonemasons to abandon their craft or look for a more lucrative way of using their skill. The Council for the Care of Churches (now the Council for Places of Worship) has done all within its power to encourage the true craftsman. But the development of machinery has enabled the production of large numbers of similar stones cheaply. These can be supplied ready-made with only the inscription to be added. The disappearance of the local stonemason has led to the increase of mail-order firms who advertise nationally but whose wares are more suitable for the cemetery than the churchyard. Choice of a gravestone demands not only knowledge of the local regulations but a sensitivity in judging the right stone and design for a particular churchyard.

Previous editors have deplored the use of white marble. In retrospect it was perhaps the shapes that were constructed from this material rather than the material itself which caused such offence. Experience has shown that some white marbles lose their shiny surface and become covered with lichen as the years pass. Nevertheless white marble is not permitted since this material, especially with any considerable degree of polish, is not sympathetic to the traditional character of the English churchyard and white marble of any variety will therefore strike the observer as a 'sore thumb' unless it is in a completely separate area of the churchyard (*e.g.* as at Long Melford, Suffolk, where the newer and quite distinct part of the churchyard has a collection of marble monuments which present a homogeneous impression of their own). An even less satisfactory innovation has been the increase in the use of highly polished black granite, often with glaring gold letters. It is unlikely that this material will ever look weathered, and its use should be firmly resisted. Plastic memorials have been subjected to practical and scientific tests and have also been found unsatisfactory on a still greater number of counts. They are easily scratched or burnt, and readily dissolved by common chemicals.

The illustrations in this new edition endeavour to show the approach of a new generation to the design of churchyard memorials, and make clear that there is no need to follow exclusively Georgian, or what is better described as classical patterns, in order to produce something of quality. It should be recognised that in order to keep in business the memorial industry has had to become highly mechanised. This, however, does not preclude the production of good designs. Figure 5 indicates that the classical vocabulary, if used with sensitivity and skill, is neither inappropriate nor moribund. Of the two examples shown one is by Laurence Whistler, widely known for his writings and his engravings on glass, and the other is by Simon Verity.

The churchyard should be the responsibility of the community and as many people involved as possible in its care and upkeep. The parish of Penn in Buckinghamshire does this excellently through a Churchyard Guild. Some parishes maintain a Churchyard Fund; others have a special Gift Day once a year for it. Bequests and donations may be invited not only from regular church members but from parishioners in general. It should, however, be made clear that such gifts are intended for the upkeep of the churchyard as a whole and cannot be earmarked for a particular grave. Parishes have sometimes found themselves committed to maintaining a particular memorial in return for a donation which, though reasonable enough at the time it was given, has been rendered wholly inadequate by inflation.

A churchyard is like a work of art and we prefer a scheme for its re-arrangement to be of the character of a restoration rather than 're-ordering' or 'improvement' when any scheme is contemplated for the re-arrangement of stones. In any case where it is proposed to do more than deal with grass, flowers and shrubs, it is necessary that the Diocesan Advisory Committee for the Care of Churches should be consulted, and a faculty obtained. The rights of all parishioners are involved and people are naturally very sensitive on the question of graves.

It is always advisable for parochial church councils to protect themselves from difficulties by adopting regulations for the control of their churchyard. We have drawn up a model set of rules for them to adopt which differs in a number of respects from the previous code. These rules are designed to limit the variety of interpretations permissible and yet to allow reasonable freedom. The exact form of regulations will vary according to individual circumstances, and also depend upon whether diocesan rules have been laid down by the Chancellor. The voluntary adoption of regulations protects the incumbent from any suspicion of arbitrariness or bias in dealing with individual applicants.

Parishes should not only conserve what is best in the historical development of the churchyard but plan wisely for future development. It may well be that, when a new section of the churchyard is opened, there should be stricter rules about the type of stone. This is especially important when a churchyard is re-used after a period of disuse and new stones will be erected near others which have been in existence for a century or more. Indeed, such an opportunity will enable a parish to consider a consistent policy from the start embracing the planting of trees and shrubs, erecting walls or fences, and the lay-out of paths, as well as laying down guidelines for the monuments.

Legal questions have been covered as far as it is practicable in a general publication of this nature, but it needs to be repeated that, although the parishioners have a right of burial, they have no right to the erection of a monument, nor has a parochial church council a duty to maintain what is in effect a parishioner's private memorial. Subject to certain reservations noted later the freehold of the churchyard is vested in the incumbent. And it should be remembered that he exercises the right to sanction erection of monuments only by custom and within limits laid down by the Chancellor: and that permission could, we believe, be withdrawn if it were to be abused.

FIG. I St Wendreda, March, Cambridgeshire. Although a tidier approach is appropriate in town as opposed to country churchyards, here it has been carried to extremes. Notice also the 'tombstones stacked round like playing cards'.
[*Photograph:* National Monuments Record]

FIG. 2   An example of beautiful and characterful lettering (and also, incidentally, a moving and direct verse epitaph) in Leicestershire slate dating from the second quarter of the eighteenth century.

[*Photograph:* Kenneth Lindley]

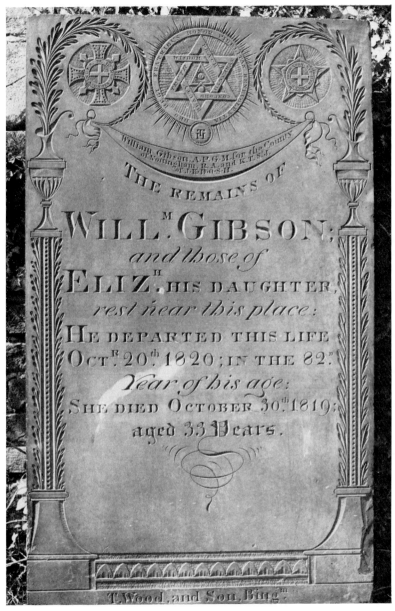

FIG. 3 A Nottinghamshire example of 'the neo-classical elegance' from Screveton churchyard, also in slate. Notice the superb quality of the deeply-cut lettering, and its excellent condition, also the signature and place-name of the mason's firm. The urns on pedestals reflect designs which emanated from the manufactories of Matthew Boulton and Josiah Wedgwood.

[*Photograph:* Mrs P. F. Heathcote]

FIG. 4   Clearly this country churchyard exemplifies a situation which could not be tolerated everywhere, especially the vegetation on and near the church itself.
[*Photograph:* National Monuments Record]

FIG. 5a A parabolic niche, with an oval base for a vase of flowers, designed by Laurence Whistler and executed by Darsie Rawlins. In Clovelly churchyard, set against the retaining wall.

[*Photograph:* Laurence Whistler]

FIG. 5b A pyramidal tombstone, based perhaps on the eighteenth-century example at Painswick, Gloucestershire. By Simon Verity.

[*Photograph:* M. B. Jones]

FIG. 6 Two admirable examples, with fine dignified lettering, of headstones essentially modern in character but adapting traditional headstone forms in good natural stone. By W. A. Hoare (Sculptors) Ltd, Bournemouth.

[Photograph: W. A. Hoare Ltd]

AUSTIN BRUCE
FERGUSON
1898 – 1972
an unassuming
courageous and most
compassionate man
greatly loved

FIG. 7 A fine headstone, developed from a traditional form by a distinguished local sculptor, in the churchyard extension at Penn, Buckinghamshire.

[*Photograph:* Darsie Rawlins]

FIG. 8   A traditional rectangular form, embellished by the carving of the achievement of arms. By Simon Verity.

[*Photograph:* O. G. Jarman]

FIG. 9   St Katherine, Loversall, near Doncaster, Yorkshire. This fine fourteenth-century tomb-chest is to be found south of the south chapel. The sides are decorated with blank tracery in patterns familiar from window designs of the same period. Note also the pleasing scale of the encircling trees on the edge of the churchyard.

[*Photograph*: National Monuments Record]

FIG. 10a

Two examples of beautiful and sophisticated eighteenth-century churchyard monuments from Painswick, Gloucestershire, noted for the fine quality of its monumental sculpture and the ninety-nine yews planted in *c* 1792. Many of the monuments were the work of a family of local carvers and masons, principally Joseph Bryan (1682–1730) and his two sons, John and Joseph.

[*Photographs:* E. Orchard]

FIG. 10b

FIG. 11   St Mary, Hambleden, Buckinghamshire: the Kendrick Mausoleum. A particularly handsome example of the churchyard mausoleum, dating from *c* 1750, beautifully related to its setting in the churchyard and the wider landscape. It is imperative that we maintain such outstanding architectural monuments in good repair, and grants may sometimes be available for this.

[*Photograph:* National Monuments Record]

FIG. 12   A superb example of an early nineteenth-century tombstone decoration, influenced directly by the engraver's art, from Screveton churchyard in Nottinghamshire.

[*Photograph:* Mrs P. F. Heathcote]

FIG. 13   A Swiss headstone, combining vivid use of a traditional symbol of the Resurrection with free lettering and robust surface treatment. Swiss cemeteries and churchyards are often remarkable for their skilful and imaginative planting, and note here the use of ground covering plants. No explanation can be given of the date of death.

[*Photograph:* Golden Hind Films Ltd]

2. History of the churchyard

Although burials associated with both pagan and Christian sacred sites and buildings have been taking place for thousands of years, the churchyard as we know it is largely a post-Reformation product. Saxon and medieval monuments do survive, some in museums and others within the church. Many of the sepulchral slabs to be seen in churches were originally in the churchyard, with a small stone set at the head and foot of the slab. Some can still be found in churchyards and should be carefully preserved. Sixteenth-century headstones are usually very small and can easily be overlooked. A particularly fine medieval monument surviving in an English churchyard is the four-teenth-century tomb at Loversall, near Doncaster (*see* Fig 9). The development of churchyard monuments in the seventeenth and eighteenth centuries is due to a considerable degree to the rise of a prosperous middle class of merchants, landowners, farmers and skilled craftsmen. The demand for churchyard monuments spread gradually down the social scale while the interiors of churches continued to receive the memorials of the most wealthy and influential families until well into the present century. The oft-quoted epitaph written by an eighteenth-century wit for his own monument at Kingsbridge, Devon, sums it up rather neatly:

> Here lie I at the Chancel door
> Here lie I because I'm poor
> The further in the more you'll pay
> Here lie I as warm as they.

The social implications of the churchyard are significant in a variety of ways. A churchyard often provides a fascinating record of English life over more than three centuries. The mere presence of a monument, however decayed, and however illegible its inscription, can be of great value to the local historian. Monuments can be dated with reasonable accuracy without recourse to inscriptions and they thus give a clue to the size and relative prosperity of a community at any given time. Local variations abound and in almost every case they provide visual evidence of local life which is available from no other

9

source. Above all the churchyard was, and ought still to be, a vivid symbol of the church's care and concern for its parishioners not only in this life but also in that beyond the grave. Within the churchyard there was ample visual evidence that the dead had been finally 'gathered in' and the tombstone was not only a marker for the body but a statement of faith in the resurrection and the glorious life hereafter. It was this attitude which dictated the use of symbolism in tombstone design and it was this aspect of the churchyard which made the nonconformists so adamant about burial within their own graveyards. In symbolic terms, therefore, the clearance of a graveyard has implications which require the fullest and most heartsearching consideration before any drastic and irreversible action is taken.

The sudden rise of the churchyard monument during the seventeenth century is in itself a matter of considerable interest. The Council for Places of Worship would be glad to know of churchyard monuments, especially those previously unrecorded, dating from before 1700, so that a central record may be kept. All such information will also be passed on to the Royal Commission on Historical Monuments. It must be remembered that throughout the seventeenth and much of the following century, the transport of stone over any but the shortest distance was so difficult and expensive as to be almost unthinkable for such purposes as graveyard monuments. It was not until the canals, and later the railways, began to make bulk transport a possibility that varieties of stone appeared in graveyards. Before the building of the canals, village communities were largely self-supporting and the stone for memorials, like that for building, would come from local quarries. The men who carved them would be local craftsmen who, certainly until the late eighteenth century, and in many cases up until much more recent times, would spend much of their lives working on the repair and construction of vernacular buildings. It seems likely that they built up a stock of gravestones in the winter months when other work was scarce, and then added the inscriptions later as and when they were required. Their skills, together with many of the designs, were handed down from one generation to another—often within the same family. When outside influences affected the life of the community, these are frequently reflected in sudden changes in tombstone design. Particularly fine examples of this can be seen in many Gloucestershire churchyards, where the charming rusticity of earlier stones was superseded by sophisticated designs of great beauty during the period when architects and masons of the highest ability were engaged in supplying the local gentry with elegant houses in landscaped parks (Fig 10). The influence of theories about the nature of landscape and the picturesque were so powerful that some who could well afford otherwise preferred an outdoor setting for their monuments—an excellent example is the mausoleum in the churchyard at Hambleden, Buckinghamshire, seen against the background of a park-like setting (Fig 11).

Not only does the churchyard display the rapid change from rusticity to sophistication in the leaders of rural society during the eighteenth century, it also reflects the spread of wealth during the same period. The influence of the 'Age of Elegance' is scarcely better displayed than it is in some English churchyards—especially when seen in a total relationship embracing great house, park, church and village. Many of the best examples of eighteenth-century design and craftsmanship can be found in what are even now remote graveyards in the deep countryside.

Earlier lettering—often delightful, but crude—was generally replaced in the eighteenth century by skilled versions of the Roman alphabet or virtuoso interpretations of pen or engraved forms. In the Midlands, the carvers of slate tombstones from the Swithland quarries were signing their work as 'engravers', and the specialised craftsman mason was beginning to appear (see Fig 12).

The second great period of churchyard memorials began with the advent of the nineteenth century. For at least the first half of the century tombstones are an invaluable source of information on local history at a time of great upheaval and social change. Midland slates travelled up the newly-opened navigations, and their inscriptions plot the dates of canal openings with accuracy. Cast-iron memorials from the Coalbrookdale foundry (the 'birthplace' of the Industrial Revolution) spread into the Shropshire churchyards as a very acceptable substitute for local stone of mediocre quality. Thus, a rusted iron monument with no legible inscription can have importance in terms of local history as well as being one of those visual details which give character to the local scene.

By the mid-nineteenth century the production of monuments had reached a peak in quantity with little diminution of quality. The old standards of genteel lettering had been replaced by a robust use of every available letter form with a sense of design allied to craftsmanship which has not since been equalled. Never before or since has cut lettering been put to better or more varied use than on the tombstones (particularly the slates) of the last century. Similarly, the old symbols were being replaced by a more varied range which was only later subdued, first by the exponents of Gothic and later by the more fertile sentimental imagery of the late Victorians. In dealing with these it is as well to remember that fashions change and that what we may dislike our children may well admire. Churchyards reveal changes in taste and fashion over the years and there is a danger of obliterating the evidence of a period whose attitudes and imagery do not happen to be in accord with our own. A considerable degree of humility is required of us when advising what stones, if any, should be permitted to be removed.

By the middle of the last century the pattern book monument had appeared. These stemmed from several sources, the combined effect of which caused the demise of local style in monuments and the initiative of local craftsmen. One was the book of 'suitable' designs, usually by respectable architects, which depicted monuments based upon medieval tombs; another the publication of tracts by the clergy, vigorously propounding standards of ecclesiastical taste and propriety. Examples are *A Tract Upon Tombstones* by the Rev. Francis Paget (1843), *A Paper on Monuments* by the Rev. John Armstrong (1844), and *A Manual of Sepulchral Memorials* by the Rev. Edward Trollope, FSA, with a dedication to and a commendation by the Lord Archbishop of Canterbury. A third was the catalogue of the newly emerged trade of monumental mason. This introduced new designs and new materials both of which had little or nothing to do with the locality in which the monuments were to be used. Thus began a trend which continues today and which has extended to include monuments of unsuitable foreign material, cut by foreign masons in foreign workshops, entirely divorced from our native tradition. Most of these are meaningless in almost every sense and they have done much to destroy the character of a large number of churchyards. It is a tragedy that they are frequently left in position when older memorials are removed in misguided attempts to 'tidy up'.

Towards the end of the last century the followers of William Morris and protagonists of the Art and Crafts movement did a great deal to balance damage done by the commercialised production of monuments. It has been the flood of ready-made imported memorials in the present century which has seemed virtually to stifle the vernacular tradition. In the years between the wars valiant attempts were made, notably by Eric Gill and his associates, to raise standards and to re-introduce native stones. Unfortunately these had insufficient effect on the overall picture and their works have an intellectual appeal which, though distinguished, was bound to be limited in its impact. What is needed today is the total rejection of mass-produced gravestones, a willingness to allow original designs (*see* Fig 13) and positive encouragement for the use of appropriate (preferably local) materials or materials which closely correspond to indigenous stones. In present conditions a monument is likely to last just as long as someone is prepared to look after it and it may be as well to encourage the use of wood—oak for preference, *e.g.* in the form of a simple cross or graveboard. It cannot be too often stressed that monuments need not be elaborate to be good. It is not only cost which has excluded local craftsmen and materials but a combination of widespread misunderstanding of the place and purpose of a monument, and the influence of salesmanship at a time of stress. Sound advice could often avert some of the horrors of contemporary graveyard design as well as ensuring fewer aesthetic or practical problems for the future. The nature of such advice is developed further in Chapter 7 on *New monuments*.

3. The archaeological value of churchyards

The churchyard, with the church itself, often provides a microcosm of the history of the settlement which surrounds it. Each ancient churchyard has reached its present form by processes of growth which can potentially be reconstructed by a study of the age and position of graves, the shape of the curtilage, and the relationship of graves and churchyard to the church. Archaeologists, moreover, are beginning to realise that churches themselves and the areas around them often contain remains of ancient buildings and the buried archaeological layers associated with them. Such ancient deposits often contain information about the origins and development of the church, of the church-yard and its boundaries, and indeed of the community itself. When the church was originally built for instance, perhaps in Saxon times, there may well have been a need for temporary lime kilns in the vicinity, as were found near the late Saxon church of Great Paxton, Huntingdon-shire. Church building projects will also have given rise to layers of stone chippings resulting from the dressing of building stone, mortar mixing areas, and often rubbish layers deposited by the builders. Similar layers may have built up at every phase of reconstruction of the church. Such deposits look insignificant enough to the layman. An archaeologist, trained to recognise their meaning, may well, however, be able to read into them history for which there is no written record. This is particularly so if he is able to recover datable objects, for instance pieces of pottery, from the layers revealed. The opportunity to consider the history of the settlement itself may come when new areas are taken in to extend the churchyard, often over the vacant sites of former ancient houses if the settlement is an old one.

In ancient churchyards chance finds may also be made from time to time of small objects which give a clue to the settlement's antiquity. A disproportionately large number of the finds of Anglo-Saxon coins of the seventh to ninth centuries have, for instance, come from church-yards. This may reflect a long-forgotten custom of the period of placing coins in otherwise Christian graves. Early Viking burials together with grave-goods, though pagan, may still have taken place in churchyards and objects of that age are therefore sometimes turned up. Any excavation in a churchyard, for whatever purpose, could therefore reveal evidence important for an understanding of the history of the church and community.

It is, of course, impracticable to call upon an archaeologist whenever a hole is dug in a churchyard. Extensive excavations are a different matter, as for instance for the laying of drains, or the preparation of areas for a car park, or for the foundations of new buildings, or for the replacement of a boundary wall, or the extension of the churchyard. An archaeologist will welcome this as an unusual opportunity to observe an area otherwise unavailable to his researches. The Council for British Archaeology (7 Marylebone Road, London NW1) has nominated an archaeological consultant for each diocese who will be glad to advise on individual cases and to arrange for observation if necessary. His address can be found in the CBA booklet *The Archaeology of Churches* or it can be obtained from the CPW or from the Secretary of the Diocesan Advisory Committee. Some general aspects of church archaeology are described in the CPW leaflet *Churches and Archaeology*.

The most important thing about individual finds made in churchyards, whether they be small objects, pottery, coins or sculptured or ornamental stones is that they should be preserved and given professional conservation treatment if necessary. Metal objects, for instance, will deteriorate quickly if left untreated. Once again, the diocesan archaeological consultant will advise. To the archaeologist it is also important that the discovery should be made known so that it can take its place in the Ordnance Survey's records of archaeological discoveries, and be added to the general body of knowledge. The object itself will be the property of the owner of the graveyard, usually the incumbent, unless it be of gold, silver, or coin of the realm, in which case it should be reported to the Coroner who may decide to make it the subject of a treasure trove inquest. Though some churches have made attractive and satisfactory displays of excavated objects it is often more satisfactory for small objects to be placed in a nearby museum, where they will receive continuing care and attention, and will not be subject to the varying interests of successive incumbents. Many an important object has been lost because, once covered in dust, its interest and archaeological value, and the circumstances of its discovery, had been forgotten.

4. Churchyards and the law*

It is impossible in a short space to give an exhaustive account of the whole of the law affecting churchyards and what follows indicates the main features, though subject from time to time to modification. In any case of doubt, legal advice should be sought either privately from a solicitor or from the Diocesan Registrar who will have the necessary specialised knowledge.

The legal ownership of a churchyard is usually vested in the incumbent; but both his own rights and his own obligations in respect of it are very limited, for churchyards are the subject of rights and obligations affecting a number of persons.

Jurisdiction over Churchyards

In the case of the ordinary parish church, the churchyard is (like the church) subject to the jurisdiction of the bishop, exercised by the chancellor in the Consistory Court. By an express provision of the *Faculty Jurisdiction Measure 1964* this applies equally to the unconsecrated curtilage of a consecrated church. As a result, in general, no alterations, whether by way of addition, subtraction or otherwise, may be effected without a faculty from the court. Thus, no electric cables or wires for lighting or heating may be laid in the ground or carried overhead without a faculty; nor, without a faculty, may pipes or storage-tanks for oil or water be installed; nor may any building be erected or removed. A faculty is also required for any substantial alteration in the layout of the churchyard, including the large-scale levelling of grave-mounds, the removal or re-siting of grave-stones, the granting of a right of way (for example, for the purpose of road-widening), the making of new paths or the removal of old ones, and the demolition or construction of walls or the substitution of one type of wall or fence for another.

In certain instances monuments in churchyards have been scheduled as ancient monuments. In such cases, not only is a faculty from the

* This summary has been prepared with the help of a sub-Committee of the Legal Advisory Commission of the General Synod.

Consistory Court required before anything may be done to the monument, but three months' notice must also be given to the appropriate Minister of the Crown (the Secretary of State for the Environment) who may make a preservation order in respect of the monument. In some instances monuments have been listed (as distinct from scheduled), and any alteration to them (including removal) may be held to require consent from the local planning authority as well as a faculty. The extent of secular control over churchyards and monuments is dealt with in greater detail later in this chapter.

RIGHT TO INTERMENT

Parishioners and persons dying in the parish have the right (through their personal representatives) to interment in the churchyard, if consecrated, if there is room, and if it has not been wholly closed for burials by Order in Council. While the legal right strictly relates to the burial of a body and not of cremated remains this distinction is of less significance since the revision of the Canons in 1969 because Canon B.38 now provides that, save for good and sufficient reason, the ashes of a cremated body should be interred or deposited in consecrated ground and imposes on ministers an obligation not to refuse burial, expressed in terms which apply equally to a corpse and to ashes. Therefore when the body of a parishioner or person dying in the parish has been cremated, the subsequent burial of the cremated remains in the churchyard, if desired, should normally follow as a matter of course. But where there is an Order in Council restricting burials in a churchyard (either by prohibiting them altogether or by making them subject to conditions), the burial of cremated remains should only take place in accordance with a faculty which may conveniently be a general faculty, *i.e.* not granted solely for one particular burial. There is, however, no right to burial in any particular part of the churchyard and, unless a space has been reserved by faculty, it is within the incumbent's discretion to choose the spot.

If it is desired to set aside a portion of the churchyard for the interment of cremated remains, and for that purpose alone, a faculty should be sought. The burial of cremated remains is dealt with in a later chapter (p. 96).

The right to burial is not confined to members of the Church of England. Subject to certain limitations as to the use of the Church of England burial service, it is the duty of the incumbent, after due notice, to conduct the burial of any parishioner or person dying within the parish. However, where there is a right to interment (that is, in the case of a parishioner or person dying within the parish), any relative, friend or legal representative has the further right to require that the burial shall take place in the churchyard either without any service at all or with a Christian (though non-Anglican) service, conducted by someone of their choosing, for example a minister of another denomination.

Burial of Non-parishioners

Although in the case of persons who are neither parishioners nor die within the parish there is no right to burial in the churchyard, permission (which may be given generally to cover a limited class or particularly in individual cases) may be given for such burial. Such permission should be sparingly granted for it infringes upon the rights of the parishioners for whose interment the churchyard is primarily intended. It is particularly important therefore to avoid giving any impression that this permission will automatically be given in return for a substantial payment. Provided, however, that ample grave space is available, there is no reason why such burials should not be allowed on payment of a suitable charge (*e.g.* a sum equal to twice the fees payable on the burial of a parishioner) bearing in mind that this payment will normally be applied towards the maintenance of the churchyard.

The permission to be sought for the burial of non-parishioners used to be that of the incumbent and churchwardens; but after the transfer from the churchwardens to the parochial church council of the duty for care and maintenance of the churchyard under the *Parochial Church Councils (Powers) Measure 1921*, the view was, and still is, widely held that it is the parochial church council rather than the churchwardens who should join with the incumbent to allow the burial of non-parishioners. The legal position is not free from doubt, but as a practical measure parochial church councils and churchwardens might agree that the incumbent and churchwardens should exercise this power while at the same time observing any general directions from the parochial church council in the light of the amount of grave space available or likely to be available. The *Church of England (Miscellaneous Provisions) Measure* at present awaiting Royal Assent contains the following clause which will clarify the position for the future when the Measure becomes law:

'No person other than a person having a right of burial in the churchyard or other burial ground of a parish, shall be buried therein

18

without the consent of the minister of the parish, but in deciding whether to give such consent the minister shall have regard to any general guidance given by the parochial church council of the parish with respect to the matter.'

In this connection it should be remembered that there are certain categories of persons who, though not strictly parishioners, may have customarily been regarded as such. In these cases no such permission should in practice be necessary and the table of fees in connection with the burial of parishioners may be applied. The Church Commissioners in the explanatory notes issued with the 1962 and 1972 tables of fees gave as examples of these categories ex-parishioners, and non-parishioners for whom family graves or vaults were desired to be opened or whose close relatives had been buried in the churchyard. To these might be added non-parishioners whose names were on the church electoral roll at the time of their death. When the *Church of England (Miscellaneous Provisions) Measure* mentioned above becomes law a person whose name is on the electoral roll of a parish at the date of his death will have a right of burial in the churchyard of the parish even if not resident in the parish.

DEPTH OF GRAVES

There is no uniform provision throughout the country about the depth of graves and there will be many churchyards where there is no restriction on this, but where there is any possibility of any restrictions being in force they should be ascertained and observed. The most common provision is that contained in Section 103 of the *Towns Improvement Clauses Act 1847* which, where it is in force, means that no coffin may be buried without at least thirty inches (750 mm) of soil between the lid and the surface of the ground. Where a churchyard or an extension has been opened with the approval of the Secretary of State for the Environment or his predecessors this has in certain cases been granted subject to compliance with regulations which provide that no coffin should be buried in an unwalled grave within four feet (1200 mm) of the level of the ground. When a churchyard has been closed by an Order in Council which contains exceptions, the Order usually stipulates a depth of not less than four feet (1200 mm) but some-times five feet (1500 mm) and the Order should be referred to. Since *circa* 1908 the normal provision has been three feet (900 mm). Finally, in some areas there is a provision in a local Act fixing a minimum depth applicable to all burial places in the area, though this is only likely to be found in urban areas.

DISINTERMENT OF BODIES

Once a body has been buried, it may not be disinterred without lawful authority. In cases where crime is suspected this may be given by the coroner. Both the *Pastoral Measure 1968* and secular planning legislation make provision for the disinterment of bodies in burial grounds affected by redundancy or planning schemes and for their reinterment elsewhere. In all other cases a faculty is required as, for example, where it is desired to remove a body from one part of the churchyard to another (because, perhaps, it was by mistake buried in the wrong grave space); and in addition to a faculty a licence is required from the Home Secretary under Section 25 of the *Burial Act 1857*, unless the re-burial is in consecrated ground.

RE-USE OF OLD GRAVES FOR FRESH BURIALS

As there is no right to burial in any particular part of the churchyard unless a space has been reserved by faculty or under the *Consecration of Churchyards Acts 1867 and 1868*, it follows that (subject to com-pliance with any requirements about the depth of graves or of any Order in Council restricting burials to relatives of those already buried in a particular grave, which may apply to that particular churchyard), there is no legal objection to burial in a grave which has already been used, even though the person to be buried is not related to any of those already buried in that grave. But clearly this could cause distress if done indiscriminately, and in practice, especially if a tombstone has been erected, further burials in a grave will usually be confined to members of the same family. There may, however, be some grave spaces where it is many years since any burial took place, or where it is known that the person buried has no surviving relatives, and where therefore it might not be inappropriate to use the grave for the burial of someone unconnected with the person or persons already buried there. This will be easier if no tombstone has been erected.

Or there might be a portion of the churchyard which has not been used for burials for many years (and which has not been closed for burial by Order in Council) where it would be appropriate to seek a faculty to remove (and possibly re-site) all the gravestones and make the ground available for re-use for burials.

Even where rights to grave spaces have been granted by faculty or reserved under the *Consecration of Churchyards Acts 1867 to 1868*, the effect of Section 8 of the *Faculty Jurisdiction Measure 1964* is that all such rights cease one hundred years after the passing of the Measure or, in the case of extensions or new grants by faculty, after the date of the faculty.

ERECTION OF MONUMENTS

Burial does not confer a right to erect a tombstone or other monument and, strictly speaking, the erection of one without a faculty is unlawful. Though the practice varies according to local conditions from diocese to diocese, it is usual today for the court to be content to leave it to the incumbent to grant permission for the erection of a simple tombstone of specified size and material, but to require a petition for a faculty for anything outside the scope of what has been specified (*see* Rules, set out in Appendix II). If the incumbent's permission is not forthcoming, it is still open to the applicant to apply for a faculty, provided he is a person with sufficient legal interest to be a petitioner. It is very unwise to place any order for a tombstone until it has been ascertained that permission for its erection will be granted and the inscription approved. In the first instance, therefore, early application should always be made to the incumbent.

FEES

Tables of fees, made by the Church Commissioners with the approval of the General Synod under the *Ecclesiastical Fees Measure 1962* (*see* the *Parochial Fees Order 1972*, S.I. 177), govern the amounts payable in respect of burials and the erection of monuments. But, in addition to these, in those cases where a faculty is sought, for example for the erection of a monument of a kind which might make it more difficult to keep the churchyard tidy, or for the reservation of a grave space, it has become customary for the court to grant such a faculty only on condition that a minimum additional sum is paid to the parochial church council to help towards the upkeep of the churchyard. Because of inflation, the sum agreed should be reviewed from time to time and indeed suggestions have even been made for an annual rental. Parochial church councils should be encouraged to establish a Churchyard Maintenance Fund for the upkeep of the churchyard, into which these sums should be paid.

CLOSURE OF CHURCHYARDS

Burial grounds may be closed for burials, wholly or subject to exceptions, by Order in Council made under statutory authority and many churchyards have been closed in this way. The appropriate Minister will not in practice advise the making of such an Order except on the grounds of public health.

Any parish seeking closure of its churchyard by Order in Council should, in the first instance, make contact with its local district council, as the views of their medical adviser are likely to be crucial. No bodies may be buried in contravention of an Order in Council but the prohibition does not extend to cremated remains which may still be interred there. Apart from this limitation on burials, all legal rights and liabilities and the jurisdiction of the Consistory Court remain unaffected, save in one important respect of which parochial church councils should more often take advantage, namely, that they may call upon the local authority to accept responsibility for the maintenance of the churchyard (*see* now the *Local Government Act 1972*, Section 215).

The former prohibition on making an Order in Council closing a burial ground which had been opened with the approval of the Secretary of State appears to be excluded by the *Local Government Act 1972*, Schedule 26, paragraph 15.

DISUSED BURIAL GROUNDS

A burial ground closed by Order in Council (whether or not subject to exceptions) is a disused burial ground, and there is a statutory prohibition against building on disused burial grounds generally. The prohibition however, does not extend to the enlargement of the church, for which purpose a faculty may still be granted. However, Section 30 of the *Pastoral Measure 1968* makes provision for pastoral schemes to effect appropriation to other uses of churchyards and burial grounds not annexed to redundant churches (to which special provisions apply) and sub-section (2) makes it clear that, in such a case, provided certain stated conditions are met, the former prohibition against building no longer applies (*see also* Appendix X on the *Pastoral Measure*). Under the *Open Spaces Act 1906* there is provision whereby a disused burial ground may be handed over to the local authority, for value or otherwise, for use as an open space. A faculty is still required before the local authority may make alterations or exercise powers of management over such a churchyard, but, subject to the terms of the faculty, tombstones may be removed and the ground laid out afresh. The open space thus acquired may, if the faculty so permits, be used for games, and tennis courts have in fact been made on some such disused churchyards (*e.g.* in the churchyard of St Botolph, Bishopsgate, in the City of London).

CARE AND MAINTENANCE

The responsibility for maintaining the churchyard in good condition rests on the PCC, save in the case of a closed burial ground, *i.e.* closed by Order in Council, where the obligation may be passed to the local authority under Section 215 of the *Local Government Act 1972*. Where the obligation existed before 1st April 1974 it will have passed to the successor local authority (*see* Article 16 of the *Local Authorities etc (Miscellaneous Provision) Order 1974*). The PCC's obligation is, of course, limited by the funds at its disposal; hence the justice of requiring a donation towards the upkeep of the churchyard as a condition of the grant by faculty of any special privilege, such as the reservation of a grave space. Section 214 (6) of the *Local Government Act 1972* empowers district and parish councils and also London borough councils and parish meetings where no councils exist, to contribute towards the upkeep of burial grounds for the interment of parishioners, and, though they cannot be compelled to contribute, PCCs might well consider asking them for a voluntary contribution (*see* Chapter 25 on Assistance from Local Authorities). Sometimes, where a local authority has assumed responsibility for maintenance, the PCC pays a voluntary contribution.

It should be noted that the upkeep of the burial ground refers to the burial ground as a whole and does not extend to the upkeep of individual monuments, such as tombstones; these remain the responsibility of those who erected them, and after their death (according to the view most commonly accepted) of the heirs at law of those commemorated. Often such persons are not interested or cannot be traced; nor is there any enforceable legal obligation on them to maintain a memorial, save perhaps in the event of its becoming so dangerously ruinous as to constitute a danger to the public. It is, however, open to anyone to give money on trust for the upkeep of the churchyard *as a whole*, though not on trust for the upkeep of a particular grave. But a gift of money on trust for the upkeep of the churchyard as a whole, so long as a particular grave is maintained, is a valid charitable gift (specimen forms will be found in Appendix V); in such a case, the donor should give or bequeath either a capital sum of at least £300, or a sum sufficient,

23

when invested, to bring in an annual income of a minimum of £15 (and, once again, these figures should be constantly reviewed in the light of inflation). The actual cost of maintaining the particular grave must be met from other sources as if it is met from the income of the Trust Fund, income tax exemption will be lost.

The maintenance of good behaviour in the churchyard falls on the churchwardens. To create a disturbance in a churchyard is still a criminal offence for which the churchwardens may prosecute before the magistrates.

OCCUPIERS' LIABILITY

Occupiers of land, and others with obligations in respect of land, always run the risk of incurring liability for damages to persons who are injured by reason of hazards on the land (for example, a fall of masonry from a wall which has been faultily constructed, or a trench which has been inadequately fenced). It is, therefore, prudent to see that the incumbent, the churchwardens and the PCC are adequately covered by insurance against the damages which might be awarded in such a case and which might well be heavy.

HERBAGE AND TREES

The incumbent has the right of herbage in the churchyard. Thus, the grass which is cut therein belongs to him. Advantage is taken of this right all too seldom, for it may lawfully be exercised by turning sheep into the churchyard, and this, when done with discretion, is an admirable way of keeping down grass. Provided damage is not done to monuments, and rights of access to the church are not prejudiced, there would seem no reason why other animals, such as tethered goats, should not be used for this purpose. Trees, however, unless dangerous, may not be felled without permission except to avoid some imminent risk. In this instance the permission is to be sought, not from the Consistory Court, but from the Parsonages Board of the diocese (or, where there is no Parsonages Board, from the Diocesan Board of Finance) under Section 20 of the *Repair of Benefice Buildings Measure 1972*. Trees in a churchyard may also be subject to Tree Preservation Orders.

USE FOR SECULAR PURPOSES

It is doubtful whether a faculty can authorise the complete alienation of a consecrated churchyard. It is certain that only statutory authority (*e.g.* the *Pastoral Measure 1968*) can deprive the Consistory Court of its jurisdiction over any consecrated land. Since it is the duty of the court to see that the land is not put to a use which is inconsistent with the act of consecration, there would seldom be any point in seeking its alienation by means of a faculty. In appropriate cases, however, churchyards have been put to some secular use by or under the authority of a faculty, where that use is of benefit to the church or the parishioners. Thus, local authorities and others have been allowed to put lamps in the churchyard and to construct paths across it, and to lay drains and pipes for gas or electric cables under it, in cases where the church or the parishioners will benefit.

In conclusion it is important to remember that bishops, chancellors, incumbents, churchwardens and PCCs are only trustees in respect of churchyards, though an incumbent has the right of herbage and the parishioners their right of burial.

SECULAR PLANNING CONTROL

General Planning Control

It may be helpful to recapitulate the extent to which *churches* in use are affected by secular planning legislation. Contrary to what is sometimes supposed, churches are subject to ordinary planning control in the same way as most secular buildings. 'Planning permission is required for the carrying out of any development of land',[1] and that 'development' includes works materially affecting the exterior of a building is clear from the fact that works affecting only the interior of a building or not materially affecting the external appearance of a building are specifically exempted.[2] In other words planning permission is required for a wide range of works to or affecting churches including:

(1) The substitution of a different form of roof-covering
(2) The alteration of the external appearance of a window, *e.g.* by the provision of double-glazing
(3) The addition of a porch or vestry
(4) The installation of an oil-storage tank so as materially to affect the exterior of a building
(5) The erection of a clock-dial
(6) The development of land for use for burial or for the deposit of cremated remains

4

But development does not include demolition except in Conservation Areas (v. *Town and Country Amenities Act 1975*). Churches in use are also exempt from the provisions of the 1974 Act. If there is any doubt, then it would be wise to seek the advice of the Planning Officer.

The 'listing' of Churches

Planning legislation has, since 1947, required the Secretary of State for the Environment or his equivalent to list buildings that are considered to be of special architectural or historic interest.[3] He employs a team of skilled investigators for that task. When a building is so listed it is normally necessary to obtain Listed Building Consent before the carrying out of any works for its demolition, or its alteration or extension in a way which materially affects its appearance. Although churches in use are exempt from listed building control,[4] the Secretary of State is nevertheless empowered to list churches, and it appears that something like 11,000 churches belonging to the Church of England have already been listed—including virtually all medieval churches. The lists are being constantly revised so that, for example, an increasing number of nineteenth-century churches are now listed. The faculty jurisdiction is the Church of England's equivalent to secular listed building control and in some respects (*e.g.* regarding furnishings, whether moveable or otherwise) it is more comprehensive and effective than listed building control. *It is vital that its provisions should be scrupulously observed.*

The listing is of some guidance to local authorities who under the *Local Authorities (Historic Buildings) Act, 1962,* may contribute towards the expenses incurred or to be incurred in the repair and maintenance of churches and other buildings of historic interest.

A local planning authority may serve a Building Preservation Notice as a temporary means of conferring the protection obtainable from listing. Alternatively they may make a direction controlling demolition. But no such notice or direction may be served in respect of an ecclesiastical building for the time being used for ecclesiastical purposes.[5]

Churchyards

The position with regard to churchyards is as for churches, except in one particular. Under the *Ancient Monuments Acts, 1913–53*, the Secretary of State is empowered to schedule ancient monuments, thereby imposing the requirement to give three months' notice of intention to demolish, alter or extend.[6] For long-term protection it is necessary to make a Preservation Order.[7] For the purpose of the Acts 'the expression "monument" includes any structure or erection, other than an ecclesiastical building which is for the time being used for ecclesiastical purposes'.[8] Churches are therefore exempted, but structures in churchyards have been considered eligible for scheduling.[9]

The Secretary of State is empowered to schedule, in addition to memorials, any of the following:

(1) Gates and boundary walls, lych-gates
(2) Sundials
(3) Architectural fragments
(4) Memorials, mausoleums, etc

It is even possible for a whole churchyard, excluding the church, to be scheduled.

The structures in churchyards may, like the churches, be listed by the Secretary of State, but the listing (unlike the scheduling) has no legal effect so long as the church associated with the churchyard is listed on its own account and is in use for ecclesiastical purposes. This is because the special status of a listed building extends to the curtilage,[10] and the curtilage of a church includes the whole of a churchyard and its boundary.

Boundary Walls, etc

With regard to planning permission, gates, fences and walls are in a special category. Their construction does not require planning permission so long as they do not exceed 3 feet 3 inches (1 metre) in height where abutting on a highway used by vehicular traffic or 6 feet 6 inches (2 metres) high elsewhere.[11] But a local planning authority is empowered to designate Conservation Areas under the *Town and Country Planning Act 1971*, Section 277 (1), and one result of designation may be a direction under Article 4 of the General Development Order whereby sundry minor operations that do not normally require planning permission cease to enjoy that exemption.[12] Under such circumstances the construction of any gates, fences and walls *would* require planning permission.

Trees

Trees are distinguished from buildings in planning legislation. Those in churchyards enjoy no special status. A local authority may make a Tree Preservation Order, and where a tree is the subject of such an Order it may not, except with the consent of the authority or under certain listed circumstances, be cut down, topped, lopped or wilfully destroyed.[13] Since the passing of the *Town and Country Amenities Act 1974* the local authority is empowered to extend protection to trees in a Conservation Area even when a Tree Preservation Order has not been placed upon them. Where consent is given a condition requiring replanting may be imposed. Where a hedge is of historic interest and consists of trees, it can also be protected by means of a Tree Preservation Order.

To sum up: The effect of the secular legislation on churchyards and tombstones or other structures in churchyards is as follows:

(i) The scheduling of a structure in a churchyard has statutory force; the listing of the same structure has no statutory force unless the church itself is unlisted.

(ii) A local authority may make a tree preservation order in respect of a tree or hedge; but may not serve a building preservation notice in respect of a memorial or wall (it is therefore essential that the faculty jurisdiction should afford protection equal to that of the secular legislation here).

(iii) A church in use may not be scheduled, but a lych-gate forming part of the same architectural composition may be scheduled.

(iv) A planning authority may refuse permission to rebuild part of a church, but they cannot prevent demolition as the prelude to rebuilding. (Where the building is secular they can both refuse permission to rebuild and refuse consent to demolish.)

REFERENCES

[1] Town and Country Planning Act, 1971, Section 23 (1).
[2] *Ibid.*, Section 22 (2) (a).
[3] *Ibid.*, Section 54 (1).
[4] *Ibid.*, Section 56 (1) (a).
[5] *Ibid.*, Section 58 (2) (a); Town and Country Planning (Amendment) Act, 1972, Section 8 (1) (b).
[6] Ancient Monuments Act, 1931, Section 6.
[7] Historic Buildings and Ancient Monuments Act, 1953, Section 11.
[8] Ancient Monuments Act, 1931, Section 15.
[9] For example, in one county alone (Staffordshire) there are 14 scheduled monuments, all of them crosses. It seems likely that the Secretary of State will use his powers in this respect with increasing frequency, to protect individual monuments or whole churchyards.
[10] Town and Country Planning Act, 1971, Section 54 (9): 'Any object or structure . . . forming part of the land and comprised within the curtilage of a building, shall be treated as part of the building.'
[11] General Development Order, 1973, Schedule 1, Class II.
[12] M.H.L.G. Circular 53/67, paragraph 11.
[13] Town and Country Planning Act, 1971, Section 60 (1) (a).

5. Gravestones

Mention was made in a previous chapter of medieval churchyard monuments. Where these survive, they should be allowed to remain *in situ* unless they require the protection of being brought indoors. Medieval churchyard monuments should not be confused with monuments, perhaps just as old, removed from inside the church by Victorian or earlier restorers, but never designed for an outdoor site. In many cases these should probably be brought under cover again. *All* medieval monuments, whatever their condition, should be carefully preserved though it may well be that their condition will dictate *where* they are to be preserved. Advice on their preservation may be sought through the Diocesan Advisory Committee or the Conservation Committee of the Council for Places of Worship.

In an average English churchyard of some antiquity the earliest monuments will probably date from the latter part of the seventeenth century, but even these are not as common as is generally believed. These earlier tombstones can at times be quite crude in execution; some even have a 'home-made' quality which adds to, rather than detracts from, their charm. More frequently, the older monuments are of the eighteenth century. To this period belong most of the classical or baroque box or chest tombs, among which is great variety of craftmanship of rare beauty and weathered texture; and also the delicately carved headstones which remain in profusion in some localities.

REGIONAL FEATURES

All over the country it is possible to trace local characteristics of the stonemasons of the district. Much of their work shows originality and freshness combined with great refinement of execution. There are the typical groups of memorials of the Cotswolds and the adjacent counties where good stone was abundant, and of Warwickshire, Leicestershire and south Derbyshire; as well as of Devon and Cornwall, where the masons produced an astonishing development of fine lettering and ornament on slabs of slate. Even the more commonplace late eighteenth- and early nineteenth-century memorials carved in Portland

29

and other stones are very worthy of preservation, as showing what could be done with moderate means and good material.

Many factors were involved in the decline of the quality of memorials produced in the nineteenth century. Some good examples continued to be produced, but generally both the quality of the stone and the skill with which it was cut degenerated. The fine stone box tombs developed into brick boxes rendered to look like stone, though some interesting examples were made of cast iron, *e.g.* as at Witham in Essex, and sometimes in the Midlands; headstones lost their ornaments; lettering of good design lingered on, but with the nineteenth century it began to lose character. Throughout the first quarter of the nineteenth century fine indoor work was being done by famous sculptors such as Chantrey, Flaxman, Westmacott and many others, yet the great English tradition died, slowly but surely, down to a period of unimaginative dullness, only to be succeeded by a never-ending flood of feeble and pretentious productions which has steadily increased until our own day.

Duty to Preserve

It is clear, therefore, that virtually all earlier churchyard monuments are worthy of careful preservation because of their originality of design and skill of craftsmanship. Many have been allowed to perish with the death of the representatives of the family concerned. Their artistic merit being now recognised, it is necessary for them to be considered as part of the cultural heritage for which the Church must accept a custodian's responsibility, although bearing in mind that they remain technically in private ownership. Their maintenance now should fall within the general upkeep of the churchyard.

Iron railings round graves have, in most cases, been destroyed. They were chiefly needed for protection from thieves, gamblers, drunkards, body-snatchers, sheep and cows, or to prevent the desecration of graves of unpopular parishioners in a rougher age. Some of the eighteenth-century railings are now of great rarity value and should be kept painted and retained. Later railings are also often worthwhile, and should not be allowed to become too entangled with ivy and briars. Where instances occur of railings enclosing areas abutting on the church and preventing much-needed access to walls, windows, damp corners and rain pipes, their removal may, on the other hand, prove necessary.

When plain brick chest tombs break up, the sides can be removed and the top slab placed upon the foundation of the tomb. However, where this is done the flat stones may eventually sink, and the grass grow over them. Sunken or crooked headstones can be reset vertically, the hole being filled with rubble well tamped down to give a firm foundation beneath the turf. Ruthless straightening is neither desirable nor necessary.

REMOVAL OF GRAVESTONES

Where overcrowding makes grass cutting difficult, a few carefully selected stones may be removed and reset in some other, less crowded, part of the churchyard. This would also perhaps provide an opportunity for removing a really fine headstone into the church porch for protection, or to feature some particular headstones. If a stone is moved indoors for protection, its original position should be made clear on a plan indicating position, orientation and size. No headstone should be removed without due consideration to its value in its natural setting. Care should be taken not to disrupt groups of family graves. A trench cut round such a group may well solve a problem here, and also serve to emphasise the family group. Serried ranks of stones round the boundaries look ugly and collect more weeds and brambles. Stones should *never* be collected against the wall of the church itself.

In Cheshire and Lancashire and parts of Yorkshire it has long been traditional to provide a thick tombstone lying flat on the ground, eventually paving over the whole churchyard. In these districts the tradition should be maintained if practicable, as the stone used was hard and enduring. This is very different, however, from the practice of laying flat a quantity of thin headstones in a district where they were made to stand upright. Aesthetically this is not desirable, and this treatment leads to their decay.

In Kent and elsewhere in the south-east of England, from late in the eighteenth century onwards, it was sometimes the custom to place an uninscribed stone between the head and footstone to protect the gravespace. These took many forms—sometimes consisting of a flat narrow piece of stone; or a semi-cylindrical or coped stone. Others look like stone coffins and in (but not peculiar to) the Home Counties, the stone was shaped in such a way as to resemble a mummified body. These 'body-stones' are of historical value and generally they should not be removed or destroyed. However, they do present difficulties in churchyard maintenance and as the majority of churchyards will only possess a few, the simplest solution is to cut a trench round the whole grave. The smaller stones sometimes found at the foot of graves ought to be retained as well as headstones. If it is absolutely essential for maintenance reasons to move a footstone it should be placed at the back of the headstone and not against the inscription. It should never be moved away from the grave and placed elsewhere in the churchyard.

GENERAL MAINTENANCE

As a general rule lettering on gravestones should not be re-cut, though it may be repainted. Cleaning is preferable, and this requires some expert knowledge since the treatment required will vary according to the nature of the stone.

Where it is desired to remove lichen or green mould from churchyard monuments, *see* Appendix IV. Detergents, soda, or soap preparations containing it, should not be used for washing stone. Moss and lichen on recumbent stones may be easily removed to make the inscription legible by covering the stone with a light coating of earth for two or three weeks, and then brushing it off. If a fractured stone or broken chest tomb is to be repaired, non-ferrous metal dowels should be used as iron rusts, expands and splits the stone in which it is bedded. Chest tombs are seldom mortared together, but if mortar is needed to repair them it should follow the general advice in Chapter 10.

In many parts of south-east England, where stone was scarce and timber plentiful, a wooden memorial was erected consisting of a framed board extending lengthwise over the grave attached to a small wooden post at each end and bearing a painted inscription. These structures, known in some places as bed-heads, in others as leaping boards, were usually painted white and lettered in black; occasionally they were surmounted by an ornamental wooden cresting; sometimes the posts had decorative finials, and sometimes a row of iron spikes was placed along the top to prevent children sitting on the edge. Being of wood and usually on the graves of the less wealthy, these bed-heads have tended to decay. Falling to pieces as they generally do through the action of the weather, their remains have frequently been cleared away as rubbish. Wherever possible, any that remain should be repaired and retained as long as they will hold together. The inscriptions were usually painted, not carved, and there is no reason why they should not be repainted if the style of the original letter is carefully copied. It is doubtful if any example remains earlier than the nineteenth century. A few were set up in remoter parishes as late as the last quarter of that century and there have been sporadic revivals of the custom; it is probable that this form of memorial represents a very ancient tradition, perhaps going back into the Middle Ages.

Much information about older churchyard monuments, together with good illustrations, will be found in books listed in the Bibliography, especially those by Frederick Burgess and Kenneth Lindley. For further advice on monuments of artistic or historic interest, and their conservation, application should be made to the Council for Places of Worship.

6.   Other stones

In addition to the cross and gravestones, many churchyards contain such valuable antiquities as ancient sundials, parish stocks, and occasionally stone coffins, moulded or carved stones, monuments, or recumbent effigies which may at sometime have been removed from the church.

Sundials on pedestals, usually dating from the eighteenth or early nineteenth century, are quite frequently found in churchyards in certain districts as, for example, in Cheshire. They may be in need of repair which will require sensitive handling; and, when excessively stained with algae, they can be cleaned in the manner suggested in Appendix IV. Treatment of their stone and iron-work is a matter for specialist advice, either through the Diocesan Advisory Committee or the inspecting architect.

Parish stocks still remain in quite a number of churchyards—they are frequently found in Cornwall. Although their historical position in the churchyard is important, and should certainly be recorded if they are moved, it is often desirable for their preservation that they should be under cover. Sometimes a special shelter has been provided, or the porch proved to be a suitable place. If this is necessary, and when thoroughly dry, they should be treated for beetle or dry rot. The iron parts can be painted with a mixture of one part raw linseed oil to four parts of turpentine, mixed with a few drops of terebene and coloured with Berlin black, after first cleaning off all rust with wire wool.

Medieval stone coffins are sometimes found lying in churchyards, where they may finally disintegrate through erosion caused by action of the weather. Wherever possible they should be placed under cover, together with any miscellaneous remains of ancient carved stonework, and it is an advantage if they can be labelled with a brief note to draw attention to their historical interest. This applies especially to the fragments of important pre- and post-Conquest sculptured crosses and monuments found all over the north of England, in the north Midlands, in Cornwall, and occasionally in other localities; and to the medieval cross slabs and hogback stones which are more widely found but are, nevertheless, rare. Even the most fragmentary or unadorned pieces should be labelled and preserved, and careful watch kept for new finds which may turn up embedded in the church or churchyard walls, built into houses and farm buildings in the village, or even on the vicarage rockery. Often such fragments are all that remains of the earliest church or preaching centre in the village; and they may afford invaluable evidence for dating the foundation of the parish church.

If these stones are exhibited in the church great care should be taken in their arrangement, and expert advice (*e.g.* from the Museums service) will need to be sought on identification and display. In some cases it may be preferable to record the stone and re-incorporate it in the church fabric. An aisle should not be a museum. In other cases, deposit in the local museum may be the appropriate solution.

It goes without saying that all such items and fragments should be listed in the Inventory.

A final word about below-ground evidence. Churchyards often contain the buried remains of earlier churches or ancient buildings, which may be encountered in almost any disturbance of the ground. New drainage trenches, the foundations for new walls or clearance for car parks in or near churchyards, are frequently the occasion for discovery of such remains, whose nature can often only be established by an experienced archaeological observer. The Council for British Archaeology has nominated a consultant for each diocese who will be pleased to advise. His name may be obtained from the Council or from the Secretary of the Diocesan Advisory Committee.

7. New monuments

Choosing a design for a gravestone is not an easy task. A headstone should be a piece of sculpture but few people have the experience of choosing let alone commissioning a work of art. It is sometimes wise to defer any decision on design or wording until the emotional stress is lightened; and every application should be treated with the utmost humanity and tact. By strict interpretation of the law no memorial should be ordered until a faculty has been granted, but in practice the jurisdiction is not enforced to this extent. The legal position is explained more fully in Chapter 4 entitled *Churchyards and the law*.

The incumbent may give permission for the erection of the great majority of gravestones, provided they are in accord with any directions specified by the Chancellor of the Diocese. Where, however, this proviso is not met and where for instance a gravestone is proposed that would diverge in material or dimensions from the Specimen Rules given in Appendix II, or where an inscription is desired which appears to the incumbent to be in doubtful taste or theologically unsound (*see* Chapter 12 on *Epitaphs*), the applicant should be informed that he must apply to the Chancellor, through the Diocesan Registrar, for a faculty giving permission to erect the proposed memorial. The applicant would be wise first to seek the advice and backing of the Diocesan Advisory Committee. Permission may, of course, be refused. This does not mean that monuments outside the specified range of the Rules should necessarily be excluded from churchyards, or at least not necessarily from *all* churchyards, nor is there intended to be a disincentive to artistic creativity, but such 'out of the ordinary' monuments do require the full authority of a faculty. An application for such permission will also mean that the Diocesan Advisory Committee will have an opportunity to advise the Chancellor.

It should be explained to monumental masons, and also to parishioners, that the design of the gravestone and the wording and type of the inscription should in every case be submitted in the first instance to the incumbent. No memorial may be erected or work carried out by a stonemason until either written permission has been obtained from the incumbent, or if the incumbent states that he does not feel it within his competence to give permission for what is desired, until a faculty is granted. Such directions serve as a proper protection for the incumbent against ill-informed criticism, and should be vigorously enforced.

In most dioceses Chancellors have now issued directions based on suggestions in the previous *Churchyards Handbook* for the guidance of incumbents, defining precisely what they may and may not admit to their churchyards without further authority. Whether there are diocesan rules or not, incumbents will find their position strengthened if their parochial church councils will adopt a series of supplementary resolutions within the scope of this handbook, a suggested model for which is presented in Appendix II. Local monumental masons who collaborate with them should be informed of the diocesan and parochial rules, and the clergy should make every effort to see that they understand and appreciate the reasons for them. Unless there are exceptional circumstances peculiar to a churchyard, the local rules should not be more restrictive than those we recommend below. Unnecessary distress can be avoided if the bereaved are encouraged, in the first place by monumental masons and sculptors, to choose a form of memorial which is likely to be acceptable and if a reasonable range of choice is permitted. One point which deserves the strongest emphasis (and which it may be helpful for an incumbent to pass on to the bereaved) is that an individually designed and well executed gravestone does not necessarily cost more than the mass-produced product.

A gravestone should be durable, and also harmonious with its setting in material, size and design. The face should be capable of taking an inscription which will remain decipherable for many years without being touched-up or re-cut. Legibility can be helped where necessary by shading the letters with a matt inconspicuous wash. The design should be such as to require the minimum of upkeep. Hence kerbs and chippings are discouraged, because of the growth of weeds and the difficulty of mowing around them. (If there is a desire to delineate the area of a grave, stones may be set level with the ground but so that the mower can pass over them.)

The environment of a new monument includes not only the walls of the church and churchyard but also the existing gravestones. A churchyard has an organic character, and in some it is possible to trace the progression of taste from the eighteenth century and earlier use of local stone, through white marble and granite to the Nabresina of today. However, the existence in a churchyard of poor design or inappropriate materials should not be taken as a precedent for the repetition of previous mistakes.

The local character should be respected. Owing to increased costs and the working out of many quarries it is sometimes more economical to obtain stone from abroad. There can be no objection to the use of foreign stone provided it is similar to local indigenous kinds. Geologically there may be little difference, for instance, between a granite quarried in Scotland, Europe or India, though there will certainly be differences in colour and mineral content. Of the Common Market countries, France, Germany and Italy (which produces the famous Baveno granite) are countries from which granite is imported. Stones generally acceptable in most parts of the country are York stone, Portland, different kinds of slate, and Nabresina which comes from Italy. White marble, reconstructed stone or plastic should never be used; and neither should black granite or all-polished granites. For an extensive list of stones see Chapter 8 entitled *List of stones for monumental work*.

A gravestone provides scale to a church. The maximum dimensions should be 4 by 3 feet by 6 inches (1200 by 900 by 150 mm); minimum 2 feet 6 inches by 1 foot 8 inches by 3 inches (750 by 500 by 75 mm). See also Appendix II, p. 110.

A base forming an integral part of the design of a headstone is permitted provided it does not project more than 2 inches (50 mm) beyond the headstone in any direction and provided that it is fixed on a foundation slab (which may be of any suitable material, not necessarily natural quarried material) which itself is fixed flush with the ground and extending 3–5 inches (75–125 mm) all round so that a mower may freely pass over it (v. Fig 14). Wherever a flush foundation of this type is used under a headstone, further below-ground foundations will be required.

The traditional memorial is a headstone. Its shape generally derives from the classical vocabulary and the styles of the period. There is, however, no reason why we should fossilise the monumental mason's craft. The flat slab or ledger-slab is also a traditional type. To circumvent the difficulty of cutting grass up to its edge, it may be mounted on a foundation set flush in the ground and projecting 3 inches (75 mm) wide on all four sides. If the ledger-slab itself were set level with the ground, water would collect and damage the surface through penetration and the edges might be chipped by the action of the mower (*see* Fig 15). The form of gravestone in the shape of an open book is to be deprecated as being out of scale.

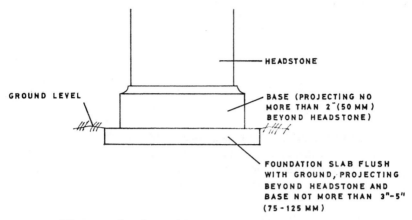

HEADSTONE

GROUND LEVEL

BASE (PROJECTING NO
MORE THAN 2″(50 MM)
BEYOND HEADSTONE)

FOUNDATION SLAB FLUSH
WITH GROUND, PROJECTING
BEYOND HEADSTONE AND
BASE NOT MORE THAN 3″-5″
(75-125 MM)

FIG. 14 Diagram to show base and foundation slab for headstones, with suggested maximum dimensions.

Restraint should be exercised in giving permission for the erection of free-standing crosses. It is easy to understand the enthusiasm with which graveyard crosses were welcomed in the nineteenth century under the influence of the Tractarian Movement, for in very many churchyards the churchyard cross had been destroyed in the sixteenth or seventeenth century, and from that time Christian symbols were rarely used outside the church building. Nothing could be more arresting than the simple cross which stood alone in the ancient churchyard. But the multiplication of smaller crosses is no help to the Christian faith and unnecessary repetition of the supreme Christian symbol may even devalue it. Crosses of good and interesting design can always be carved or incised on the face of a headstone (see Fig 16), or upon a long low ledger stone. The incumbent should require that a faculty be sought and the Diocesan Advisory Committee consulted whenever he receives a request to place a headstone in the form of a cross, especially if there is already a parish cross in the churchyard.

It is a natural desire to put flowers on a grave and some parishes have in recent years encouraged the practice of 'grave dressing' (cf well dressing). In order to prevent damage by the mower flowers should be placed in unpolished aluminium containers flush with the ground. The 'lawn-type' stone is very popular. This is a headstone on a plinth into which is incorporated a vase. Sometimes the vase is at the side. Aesthetically it may not be right to have a work of art which is incomplete in itself and dependent upon the insertion of flowers. Moreover, it is impossible to have flowers displayed throughout the year and it is rare for a grave to be tended for more than one or two generations. Generally speaking this seems to be a type of memorial more suitable to the public cemetery than the churchyard. The suggestion has been made that such types of headstone should have a stone stopper for placing over the vase hole when flowers are no longer displayed.

Related to the design of the gravestone is the manner of carving the inscription and the design of the lettering. Advice is given elsewhere about the composition of epitaphs. Care should be taken that the inscription is proportionate to the size of the stone. In many cases the arrangement of the wording is the only adornment that is necessary (*see* Fig 17). The use of the alphabet derived from the letters on Trajan's column is certainly to be encouraged; but there are other alphabets of virtually every period which could well be used more often. Leaded lettering is mechanical and dull and the lead is often pilfered. If there is any desire to tint letters, they should be painted a shade darker or lighter than the colour of the stone, but never gold.

The most usual decoration on gravestones is a rose or some other flower with sentimental associations. This is a pity, because there is a wide field of decoration as yet unused whereby the trade or the business of the departed may be commemorated. It is easy to think of the pen for the writer or the ship for the sailor; but there is also the plough for the farmer and the mallet for the mason. These are better if simplified and stylised rather than directly representational (*see* Fig 18).

Stones are supplied to the mason either sawn or partly sawn. There are a variety of obtainable finishes, rustic, sawn, rubbed, fine rubbed, polished and textured. Only one face of a memorial should be polished and that is the face where the inscription is to be engraved. Any other face or faces, or shapes, must receive a different treatment. Some masons have developed the art of varying the texture of stones with great effect and their hand-carved decorations are much to be preferred to those provided ready-made. It is not essential to polish granite in order to engrave an inscription; but where this method is employed only that face of the stone should be polished where the inscriptions are to be engraved.

In some churchyards a simple white painted wooden cross is put only a grave; in others there are more sophisticated designs in plain pecies

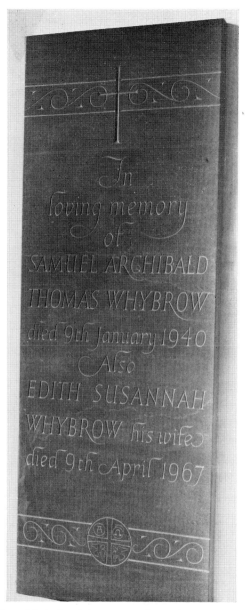

FIG. 15 A ledger slab, before being mounted on a broader foundation slab laid flush with the ground, made of finely rubbed green slate which lends itself well to the calligraphic style of lettering and decoration. By W. A. Hoare (Sculptors) Ltd, Bournemouth.

[*Photograph:* W. A. Hoare Ltd]

To face page 40

FIG. 16   A simple cross has been incorporated in the design of this headstone in riven Welsh slate made for the churchyard in Thoroton, Nottinghamshire, by John Skelton.

[*Photograph*: John Skelton]

FIG. 17   The different forms of lettering and the arrangement of the words are only two of the pleasing factors lending distinction to this headstone. Note also the flowing outline of the shape, original yet diverging little from the traditional form.

The decorative elements (a carved sheaf on the obverse and low reliefs on the reverse face) make it clear that the man commemorated was a farmer. In Bibury churchyard extension, Gloucestershire. By Simon Verity.

[*Photograph:* M. B. Jones]

FIG. 18   Here is another example of beautiful and carefully spaced lettering, with the stylised lyre representing Kathleen Coleridge-Taylor's activities as a musician. Made of Blue Hornton stone by John Skelton and placed in the churchyard of Kingston, near Lewes, in Sussex.

[*Photograph:* John Skelton]

There does not seem much enthusiasm for the eighteenth-century 'bed-head'. A good example of this type, which can be very pleasing, is to be found in the churchyard of the old church of Shenley in Hertfordshire which is a few miles from St Albans. Although wooden memorials have not the permanence of stone, many will last for two generations or more.

In the 1972 revised Scale of Fees it is stated that a 'vase' commands a fee. It is assumed that this refers to a vase with an inscription. Prior permission for the placing of such a vase should be obtained in writing from the incumbent. Such vases should not be more than 12 by 8 by 8 inches (300 by 200 by 200 mm) and must be of a natural quarried material. Their portability presents the problem of their being replaced, if disturbed, on the right grave.

Masons should not advertise their products by carving their names too prominently. Previous editions of the Handbook have opposed any signature at all on headstones. However, we believe it is a good practice for the name or colophon of the craftsman or firm to be incised in unpainted and unleaded letters no larger than $\frac{1}{2}$ inch (15 mm) in height, on the reverse or the side of the headstone. This change of policy will, it is hoped, prevent the bad mason hiding under the cloak of anonymity and encourage the good mason's work to be admired. In very large churchyards there may be a case for the grave reference number to be carved in a similarly inconspicuous way.

8.   List of stones for monumental work

This list has been prepared in consultation with geologists, monumental masons, and architects. It makes no claim to be exhaustive, but includes a sufficient variety of suitable stones to provide examples of those which may be found to be satisfactory in churchyards.

Many suitable stones may be available within a limited distance from a quarry, but several of these are only quarried intermittently, and others are subject to long delays. The only British stones which at present are not only suitable but readily available on a national basis are Portland, York and the Devon and Cornish granites. In making a choice local experience is an invaluable guide, and advice may be sought from a regional officer of the National Association of Master Masons whose name and address may be obtained from their Head Office at 37 Soho Square, London, W.1. The inclusion of any stone on this list is no guarantee of its availability and current quality. Up-to-date information may be obtained through the Federation of Stone Industries, at the same address.

Key to designations used below:
(a)   Of reliable quality and readily obtainable
(b)   Of reliable quality, but difficult to obtain
(c)   Not suitable in polluted atmospheres
(d)   More suitable for indoor than for outdoor memorials

Limestones
Derbyshire
DERBYDENE, or DERBYSHIRE FOSSIL (Carboniferous: Carboniferous Limestone). A crinoidal limestone able to take a polish and varying in colour from light to dark grey. (b)
HADENE (Carboniferous: Carboniferous Limestone). A crinoidal limestone. (b)

Dorset
PORTLAND (Jurassic: Portland Beds). A fine to medium-grained oolitic limestone with varying amounts of shell fragments, buff in

colour, weathering to a silvery white colour when washed by rain. Highly resistant to the effects of polluted atmosphere. In practice the quarried blocks are described as Whit bed or Base bed, according to whether they carry much or little shell, irrespective of their original position in the quarry. The coarse-textured Roach bed has excellent weathering qualities. It is not suitable for memorials carrying fine carving or lettering, but is well suited for use as base courses and for monumental work of a rugged character. (b)

PURBECK (Jurassic: Purbeck Beds). Coarse grained, fine grained, shelly, grey, cream, buff and blue. Easily obtainable locally. (a)

Leicestershire

KETTON (Jurassic: Inferior Oolite; *Lincolnshire Limestone*). A medium-grained oolitic limestone of even texture, notably free from shell fragments. Varies in colour from cream to pink and generally shows a high degree of durability, but is prone to deteriorate if it absorbs soluble salts from the soil, and is not suitable for headstones in areas of high pollution. (b) (c)

Lincolnshire

ANCASTER STONE (Jurassic: Inferior Oolite; *Lincolnshire Limestone*). A fine grained oolitic limestone, buff or pinkish in colour, weathering to a lighter tone when exposed to rain. Suitable for memorial tablets, but not recommended for recumbent slabs. (d). Freestone not suitable unless carefully selected.

Northants

WELDON (Jurassic: Inferior Oolite; *Lincolnshire Limestone*). A brownish-grey oolitic limestone with only small amounts of shell. May be considered too soft for monumental purposes.

Oxfordshire

BLUE HORNTON (Jurassic: Lias). A fine-grained limestone, with good weathering qualities, bluish-green in colour. (b)

BROWN HORNTON (Jurassic: Lias). The brown variety of Hornton stone is less durable than Blue Hornton. It has given fairly good service in churchyards in its own locality, but does not wear well in a polluted atmosphere. Blue Hornton is therefore generally to be preferred. (c)

Rutland

CLIPSHAM (Jurassic: Inferior Oolite; *Lincolnshire Limestone*). A shelly oolitic limestone buff or buff with blue patches, which is quarried from beds that yield stone of widely varying character. Since there is no regular sequence of beds of uniform quality, each block must be chosen on its merits. The high reputation of this stone for building work is attributable to the good weathering qualities of the hard and predominantly shelly blocks so that it is considered to be less suitable for monumental work.

Somerset

DOULTING (Jurassic: Inferior Oolite). A coarse-grained stone, consisting mainly of derived crinoidal detritus limestone, weathering to a greyish tone. Weathers poorly; not suitable for use in heavily polluted atmospheres or for recumbent slabs. (c)

Wiltshire & Somerset

BATH STONE (Jurassic: Great Oolite). A medium-grained oolitic limestone, buff in colour. Varieties such as Monks Park or Hartham Park are susceptible to damage by frost, but can be used indoors or in walls out of doors. (d)

SANDSTONES

Only a small number of sandstones are listed here. It is not necessary, for example, to know the geological names of the many different Yorkshire sandstones since monumental masons would rely on a known reputable quarry or merchant and order 'best monumental quality York stone'.

Cheshire

KERRIDGE (Carboniferous: Coal Measures). Greenish-grey; with thin darker bands. (a)

Cumbria

LAM HILL (Trias: Bunter). Mottled; brown and grey. (a)
LAZONBY (Permian: Penrith sandstone) Dark red. (a)
ST BEES HEAD (Trias: Bunter). Dark red (Bottom bed banded). (a)

Derbyshire

ENDCLIFFE (DARLEY DALE) (Carboniferous: Millstone Grit. Pinkish- and yellowish-brown. (a)
HALL DALE (DARLEY DALE) (Carboniferous: Millstone Grit; *Kinderscout Grit*). Pink, fine-grained. (b) (c)
LUMSHALL (Carboniferous: Millstone Grit). Pinkish- and yellowish-brown. (a)

Co. Durham

DUNHOUSE (Carboniferous: Coal Measures). Similar to DOD-DINGTON. (a)
HEWORTH BURN (Carboniferous: Coal Measures). Light bluish-grey. (a)

Gloucestershire, S. Wales

BLUE PENNANT (Carboniferous: Coal Measures). Blue-grey, fine-grained. Good for flat stones, but not so good for headstones. (a)

Lancashire

WOOLTON (Trias: Lower pebble beds). Red. (a)

Northumberland

BLAXTER (Carboniferous: Carboniferous: Limestone Series). Warm cream colour, hard, coarse-textured, micaceous. (a)
DODDINGTON (Carboniferous; *Fell Sandstone*). Purplish-grey. (a)
GREENLAW (Carboniferous: Cementstone group). White and fine-grained and micaceous. (b) (c)

Staffordshire

GRINSHILL (Triassic: Keuper Sandstone). Close-grained: whitish-grey.

Yorkshire

BOLTON WOOD (Monumental quality) (Carboniferous: Coal Measures; *Gaisby Rock*). Light greenish-brown, fine-grained. (a)
CROSLAND HILL (Carboniferous: Coal Measures) Yellowish-brown. (a)
ELLAND EDGE (Carboniferous: Coal Measures). Greenish-brown. (a)
GREENMORE (Carboniferous: Coal Measures). Fine-grained, blue-grey. (a)

HARD YORK. 'SILEX' (Carboniferous: Coal Measures; *Elland Flags*). Light yellowish-grey. (a)

LAND HEAD (Carboniferous: Coal Measures; *Elland Flags*). Fine-grained, brown, blue, and brown and blue.

PATELEY BRIDGE (Carboniferous: Millstone Grit). Warm grey, coarse-grained. Unsuitable for fine work, but very effective when boldly treated. (a)

WOODKIRK (Monumental quality) (Carboniferous: Coal Measures; *Thornhill Rock*). Also known as: Morley, Middleton, Robin Hood, Oulton. A fine-grained sandstone, blue or brown. (a)

SLATES

Some kinds of slate, particularly those from North Wales, have a reputation for durability. All slates are capable of taking fine lettering, but not all are suitable for use in polluted atmospheres or in salt-contaminated soils.

Cumbria

NORTH LANCASHIRE blue slate. (a)

CUMBERLAND & WESTMORLAND (Ordovician: Silurian). Varying shades of green. (a)

Cornwall

DELABOLE (Devonian) Warm grey. (a)

North Wales

NORTH WALES (Cambrian: Ordovician: Silurian). Varying shades of blue, purple, grey and green. (b)

GRANITES

Cornwall & Devon

The granite masses of:
LANDS END
CARNMENELLIS (Penryn)
ST AUSTELL   Generally medium to light grey. (a)
BODMIN
DARTMOOR

46

Cumbria

SHAP. Red with large crystals of feldspar. (a)

Scottish

Unfortunately such excellent granites as Creetown, Rubislaw, Kemnay and Peterhead are no longer available: but imported granites and other igneous rocks are obtainable.

FOREIGN STONES

Britain does not produce a large number of stones which are readily available and of 'monumental' quality, that is of a reasonable size without flaws and suitable for carving and lettering. Foreign stones, of appropriate colour and texture for the context in which the material will be placed, may therefore provide a suitable alternative. Examples include the beautiful and durable limestones of Italy (*e.g.* Nabresina and Boticino), certain Portuguese stones, and the imported stones such as those traditionally used by the Scottish granite industry. As is said elsewhere in this *Handbook* the question of appropriateness of context is all-important in deciding what material to use in a particular situation.

9. Epitaphs

Epitaphs are an ancient literary form. The best are both moving and delightful, because strong feeling or serious intent have in them found perfect expression. It is a matter of style, and the composer of an epitaph must not only know exactly what he wants to say but how to say it as concisely as possible. The longest epitaph is short compared with a newspaper obituary, so it cannot afford to contain any but essential words. Mourners should never be encouraged to lengthen an inscription into vapidity with pious sentiments, merely for the look of the thing, or for a fancied seemliness. Every word must tell, and will only do so if it is necessary and sincere. Equally, mourners should not be required to say less than they want to. It is as hard to say in principle what is the proper length for an epitaph as what is the proper length of a piece of string. These considerations ought to be borne in mind, even when the epitaph to be composed will, like the vast majority, do little more than record a name and a date.

The objects of a modern epitaph will usually be some or all of the following: to identify the resting place of the mortal remains of a dead person; to honour the dead; to comfort the living; to inform posterity. In the past two other objects have occurred: to edify the reader, usually by reminders of the inevitability of death and judgment; and to boast of the wealth, breeding or lofty family connexions of the dead. Nowadays we lack the self-confidence to carve a sermon, however brief, on a tombstone; and, it is to be hoped, no longer care to immortalise our snobbery. The other four objects are legitimate enough. In sanctioning them an incumbent cannot offend conscience. He must hope that his influence will protect the dead and the mourners alike from faults of taste, but canons of taste cannot be made as strict as the rules of grammar. The wise priest will, when in doubt, err on the side of charity, for epitaphs are expressions of love, and as such even some of the silliest may be respected. Accordingly it should very seldom be necessary to forbid an inscription outright, and it is reassuring to know that even then mourners can apply to the Consistory Court for a faculty, if they do not accept the incumbent's ruling or that of the Diocesan Advisory Committee.

48

In the present century the art of writing epitaphs has almost wholly died out in England. This is partly because of the rise in the cost of inscriptions, but chiefly because of a morbid desire to avoid the excesses of the past, when epitaphs were too often wordy and insincere. As a result, our burial-grounds are becoming deserts of verbal, as well as visual, banality. This can be to no-one's advantage. Not for nothing is one of the best-loved poems in the language entitled *Elegy in a Country Churchyard*. The consecrated ground of a churchyard, like a church itself, should be a reverenced place, where everything should, as much as possible, enrich the spirit. In this process epitaphs have their part to play.

Practicalities first. A certain minimum of information is necessary. Full name, without abbreviation: 'John William Brown', not simply 'John Brown' or 'J. W. Brown'. He must not be confused with others of like names. When the inscription relates to more than one person, it should read 'Mary Jane, his wife', or 'Mary Jane, his wife, and Jane Anna, their daughter', to avoid repeating the surname. If the wife dies first, it should read 'Mary Jane, wife of John William Brown'. However, if the husband is likely to be commemorated later on the same tombstone it should read 'Mary Jane Brown (dates)' to be followed eventually by 'and her husband John William Brown (dates)'. Dates of birth and death should be put in the most unambiguous form possible: 'Born 21 May 1901, Died 7 July 1968' is absolutely sage, in a way that variants 'Died July 8, 1968, aged 67 years' are not. Roman numerals (MCMLXXIV) may be troublesome to decipher, but are much more beautiful than arabic numerals on inscriptions.

A few other points must command general agreement. Advise against expressions such as 'Fell asleep' for 'died' unless they make a special point, like the Salvation Army officer who, said his epitaph, was 'promoted to glory'. It is absurd, in a churchyard of all places, to shrink away from the fact of death. An epitaph is a public document, and not a cosy one at that. Nicknames or pet-names ('Mum', 'Dad', 'Ginger') inscribed in stone, would carry overtones of the dog-cemetery unsuitable for the resting place of Christian men and women. When a Biblical text is used it is quite superfluous to give the reference. 'Until the day dawn (2 Pet. i.19)' is not only unnecessary, and therefore inelegant: it distracts attention from the message to the form of what is said. The Psalms should be quoted from the Book of Common Prayer, as the most familiar version; all other biblical texts should surely come from the Authorised Version, the most splendid well of language at our disposal. But it is not necessary to confine choice to the Bible. Felicitous quotations from the Prayer Book, hymns or secular sources, poetry or prose, are wholly acceptable, so long as they are truly felicitous and (in the case of the latter) consistent with Christian belief. To make sure that they are it is always prudent to check their context. Original epitaphs should also be considered.

Mourners must supply the mason with a transcript of the exact wording, lettering and punctuation which they require, and impress on him that it is not to be departed from without the incumbent's authority. On the form of lettering, and the arrangement of the composition as a whole, the advice of the mason should be sought. Lettering should be uniform in style—*i.e.* not partly Roman and partly Old English; though it need not be uniform in size, and capitals, lower case and italics may be mixed, provided they are all of the same style or 'fount', as printers call it. The wise incumbent will acquire some knowledge of the aesthetics of typography, since notably well-arranged and lettered inscriptions add much to a churchyard. The name may with advantage be larger than the rest of the text. To preserve legibility, lettering may have two coats of paint, the second coat not black but a shade darker or lighter than the stone.

If observed in the proper spirit, these principles will put those concerned on the fair road to composing a decent epitaph. But they may be ambitious to do more. If so, they must rely chiefly on their own sense of what is fitting and right. An experienced priest will have good advice to give, and, even more important, will know how to offer it acceptably. What follows is only a suggestion of what should be borne in mind.

Honour the dead   Nowadays an epitaph need not, therefore should not, aim at the completeness of an adequate obituary. The particulars of any notable career will be better preserved in the back numbers of the Press, whether national or local, or in the countless records that society today amasses. A maker of epitaphs should seek chiefly to evoke the salient points of a man's character, and only those achievements and honours which bring that character to life needing to be mentioned. This can be done in various ways. For example, when Lord and Lady Glenconner wanted to commemorate their son Edward, who was killed in the battle of the Somme, they quoted from an eye-witness account of his conduct in battle: 'When things were at their worst he would go up and down in the trenches cheering the men, when danger was greatest his smile was loveliest.' This carries much greater conviction than a more timid and conventional way of recording the young man's gallantry could have. On the other hand, sometimes the plainest statements ring truest, as with John Cook of Sutton, Cambs., who died aged 74 years having been, we are assured, 'many Years a respectable Collar and Harness maker of this Parish'. This is much better than the condescending assurance that John Parr 'was ranger of Durham Park, under the NOBLE EARL of Stamford and Warrington, for thirty-three years, which Situation he filled with credit to himself and Satisfaction to his Noble employer'. But it is easy to believe, of all three men, that they did their duty in their generation.

Boasting and snobbery being unseemly, it is best to omit all official honours and distinctions save the very highest, which it would be both misleading and mock-modest to leave out. Titles which form part of a man's name, like a knighthood or a peerage, should normally be included, on the same principle which suggests the advisability of including a man's trade: it makes him easier to identify. Edward Elgar's tomb tells us simply and sufficiently that he had the Order of Merit and was Master of the King's Musick. With equal dignity William Peach of Repton is identified as the village blacksmith.

When the titles and professions are included it is important to get them right. The proper form for a clergyman is 'John Smith, Priest' (the acceptable alternative, 'Clerk in Holy Orders', is perhaps a little precious). Dignitaries and grandees may be treated quite as economically: 'James, Earl of Radburne', not 'The Right Honourable James', etc (but 'Sir Julian Long, Baronet', not 'Julian Long, Baronet'). Common qualifications such as MA, FRICS and the like should rarely appear in an epitaph. Distinctions conferred by the Sovereign should of course be included. The rule to observe, as always, is economy. Nothing immaterial should appear on a tombstone.

Comfort the Living This is surely the most deeply-felt purpose of epitaphs—hence the innumerable affirmations that the dead are safe in heaven, the proclamations of loving grief: hence indeed the whole impulse to tend graves and to honour the memories of the departed with tombstones and inscriptions. A Church which has given the world the infinitely consoling Order for the Burial of the Dead cannot, in charity, be too restrictive in the advice it gives to mourners who wish to discharge their feelings in epitaphs. Indeed it probably ought to encourage them. Tombstones weather so quickly that they cannot, in the eye of eternity, seem appreciably more durable than paper or wood; and among the epitaphs that survive from the greatest age of English inscriptions, the seventeenth century, are many which still ring true—which still, in the richest sense of the word, endure—precisely because they were unselfconscious outpourings of deep feeling.

> . . . I'll visit thee, and when I leave this light
> Come spend my days in the same cell of night
> Where thou art lodged, and Love shall Death enforce
> To recompense the wrong of our divorce.
>
> (St Mary's, Stafford)

This, from a husband to a wife, was the best honour that could be paid her, and the best possible comfort to the husband, and makes, in every sense, the best reading for posterity. The twentieth century cannot reasonably hope to be so eloquent, but there is no cause for it to be tongue-tied.

True, there are dangers. The wise incumbent will wish to protect mourners and dead alike from solecisms; and he may see his way to discourage the use of cliché. The Authorised Version alone is so full of appropriate matter that it is depressing, and ultimately unconvincing, to come across the same half-dozen texts again and again. The same holds true of stock phrases such as 'the dearly beloved wife'. Sincerity cannot well convey itself through worn-out language. But this point should not guide conduct too strictly. Nothing could be more unfortunate than wrangling over matters of taste, at the very graveside, when the purpose of the enterprise is consolation. If mourners insist on clichés, they must have them.

Inform Posterity To a great extent this object has been covered by what has been said of the others, but it deserves a few further words. In the past the oddest things have been recorded on tombstones (probably because that was the only way they could be chronicled at all), though few match the case of John Carter of Lambourn, Berks., who was hanged for arson. At his wish his tombstone records the fact 'as a warning to his companions and others who may hereafter read this memorial'. Undeniably this and many other naïve inscriptions now give great pleasure, but we live in a sophisticated age, and an incumbent will naturally want to prevent absurdities. This granted, it remains true that the desire to commemorate remarkable events in this way is a human one, which can add greatly to the interest and value of epitaphs. So, if modern mourners, like their ancestors, want to chronicle outstanding incidents on a memorial ('She was born on the great ocean in a Storm!' says a monument at Henbury, near Bristol) they should not necessarily be discouraged.

The Golden Rule   The golden rule is the usual one. The priest should always ask himself whether he would care to be commemorated, or to commemorate others, in a given form of words: he should also ask himself if he would *seriously* object.

10. Maintaining the churchyard

The principal elements of the English churchyard are grass (including wild flowers, and lichens), trees and gravestones. Grass may be treated in a variety of ways. It may be cut in different lengths in order to provide a contrast within the churchyard. Paths or path-sides need cutting short while some parts may be kept at medium length and others allowed to grow long. A medium-length grass will permit the close approach of a mower and prevent trouble with the beards which appear around the base of stones when the grass is closely cut. There are three chief reasons why an obsessive concern with tidiness is out of place in a churchyard: economic, aesthetic, and ecological.

Grass Cutting

Lawn-like Areas: In the vast majority of cases there is no point in attempting to keep the whole area of churchyard grass in lawn condition. It is nevertheless desirable for some areas to be kept mown, if only two or three feet (600 mm or 900 mm) wide on either side of the main paths, so that long grass will not hang over the paths when wet. These and any other areas maintained as lawns will need cutting once a week, the machine being set at ¾ inch (20 mm). 'Scalping' encourages rosette weeds such as daisy and plantain and these give grass an unattractive 'herby' quality. When grass is cut at the frequency recommended there is no great bulk of clippings so that they may be left to fall. The only snag is that the cuttings may be carried into the church on feet.

Cylinder mowers where the cutters revolve in a vertical plane give the best finish. Cheaper side-wheel machines are adequate and indeed are preferable when regular cutting cannot be guaranteed. Unlike roller mowers they do not have a front wood roller which pushes down the grass before it enters the cutting cylinder. Side-wheel mowers, however, will not trim right up to edges. Rotary mowers, where the cutters revolve in the horizontal plane, can cut longer grass and even grass which is wet. They do not leave the best finish and can cut in to the soil on uneven ground. Only the more expensive models of this type have facilities for collecting grass in a box at the time of cutting.

A grass sweeper is an inexpensive and useful investment, as it can also be used for clearing leaves and other debris from the paths. The use of a gang-mower is to be deprecated in an area containing gravestones since they will inevitably become chipped or splintered.

Infrequently cut Areas: The following paragraphs refer to areas where mechanised cutting is difficult because of gravestones or other structures; areas laid aside for the conservation of native grasses; bulbs and wild flowers, and areas not yet used for burial which could provide forage for a local farmer.

There is little point in taking the first cut before the grasses have flowered. This is partly because native grasses are most beautiful in the flowering stage but mainly because it enables the main growth for the year to be removed in a single burst of effort. It also gives a heavy yield of grass (though not of the best quality) in a condition where it is most easily made into hay. The flowering state of most grasses is reached somewhere around mid-June. The first cut can be taken at any time around this date. Since there must be variation over the country the best idea would be to watch the local farmers and cut down when they are cutting their hay crops. The second growth which is known as aftermath should be cut in September. Alternatively, the second growth can be kept down by mowing at four or six-weekly intervals with a machine capable of tackling long grass.

The height has no significance in infrequently cut areas and must be governed more by the capabilities of the machines available. The cut material will generally be too heavy to leave as there would be a danger of it killing the sward by smothering. It must, therefore, be removed and made into hay, compost or be burned.

Reciprocating blade mowers of the 'autoscythe' type are very good for tall, stemmy grass. They are not too handy for use among gravestones and kerbs. To be realistic, however, there are no machines suited to this situation and resort will usually have to be made to sickles, scythes and shears. Rotary mowers will deal with grass up to six–nine inches (150–225 mm) in height. Large 'unused' areas suitable for hay can be cut with any farm mowing machine.

GRAZING

Of the normal farm livestock likely to be available, sheep appear to be the most suitable for grazing in churchyards. They are, however, very selective grazers and cannot be expected to 'pull down' tall, rough, overgrown herbage. They are unlikely to damage shrubs and young trees unless kept in an area of the churchyard for too long a period. They are also unlikely to disturb stones and kerbs by treading and rubbing. Their dung is not objectionable as it is dry and breaks up rapidly. One occasionally sees rare and ornamental breeds, such as the biblical Jacob's sheep, and these look delightful in a churchyard. Goats, though more likely to out-rank overgrown herbage, could do serious damage to valuable trees and shrubs. They need to be tethered. Cattle, whether dairy or beef, would normally be too large and clumsy for use in churchyards. Also, their dung is soft and copious. Nevertheless, they will 'pull down' rank grass better than sheep. Geese are excellent grazers. A small flock would keep the grass in an average churchyard in a lawn-like condition. They will not damage trees or larger shrubs but they do eat flowers and bulbs. Their droppings are somewhat objectionable and their hissing and neck-stretching could be off-putting to some.

Sheep, being selective grazers, prefer short, fine grass. It is essential therefore to turn them in to graze early in spring before the grass gets too tall. If the grass has become neglected, it must be mown down or eaten off with cattle first. It is unlikely that sheep could be given full-time access to the churchyard. Gates are frequently left open and cattle grids are expensive. It would be best, therefore, to graze on the 'on-and-off' basis, *i.e.* a large flock (relative to the size of the churchyard and the amount of herbage available) should be put in to graze the grass down quickly before being removed. This technique should then be repeated as soon as the grass has regrown. This grazing system results in less selectivity and, by removing the sheep as soon as the grass is eaten down, they are less likely to attack shrubs or young trees or eat poisonous weeds. The interval between grazings should be about three weeks. Cattle are not really suitable for use in churchyards but if no alternative is available, they should be grazed in the same way, *i.e.* a quick graze down followed by a rest. Intervals between grazing could be a little longer, say four weeks, as cattle can cope with taller growth.

A very large number of common and rare plants have been listed as causing death by poisoning in humans and livestock over the years. The most common species to avoid, however, are: Mares tails, (Equisetum), hemlock and other members of the Umbell family, nightshades and other members of the potato family. All these species might well be found in churchyards up and down the country. Among trees, yew is notoriously poisonous as are also the seeds of the laburnum.

COMBINATIONS OF TREATMENTS

There is no need for a hide-bound approach, namely that the churchyard must always be cut or always grazed. A labour-saving arrangement would be to leave the grass in spring to grow to the hay stage. Then after a great (but short) effort with many hands this can be cut and removed. When it has recovered, a flock of sheep could graze it down quickly in about three weeks and this could be repeated for the remainder of the season. This technique would allow spring bulbs to die back naturally and allow many wild flowers to bloom and set seed. The half-season of sheep grazing would improve the grass and thicken up the sward.

FERTILISERS

In agriculture fertilisers are used to supply elements which are essential to plant growth in situations where there is not sufficient natural return of these in the dung and urine of grazing animals. This situation will apply in many churchyards. However, except in the comparatively rare instances where churchyard grass is used for hay production or grazing, the increased growth resulting from fertilisers only accentuates labour problems associated with the cutting and disposal of grass. Fertilisers must, nevertheless, be considered.

Frequent mowing of lawns especially where clippings are boxed results in the removal of essential minerals, especially nitrogen and potash. At the same time, by restricting top growth, deep rooting is prevented and thereby the ability of the plant to remove minerals from the lower levels of the soil. The grass plants are then weakened and their ability to compete with and keep out weeds is reduced.

A deficiency of nitrogen causes the grass to become yellow in colour. A spring dressing of a 20:10:10–type compound fertiliser in spring at $2\frac{1}{2}$ cwt per acre* will help to keep the grass a good green colour and relatively free from weeds. Subsequent small dressings of nitrogenous fertiliser at $\frac{1}{2}$ oz per square yard (15 grams to 1 square metre), say two or three more during the season, will maintain the grass in a good appearance.

It is clearly not logical to apply any fertiliser to grass which is allowed to mature in situations where no utilisation as hay or grazing

* Approximately 1 oz per sq yd or 30 gms per sq m.

is possible. On large areas not yet used for burial and therefore suited to cutting for hay crops, a general fertiliser could be used in spring to improve the yield and quality of the hay. Grazed areas could be treated similarly.

HERBICIDES

There is little doubt that we have been conditioned into thinking that the presence of broad-leaved weeds is an indication of neglect and untidiness. A pure stand of grass allowed to grow rank can be just as indicative of neglect and be less beautiful or aesthetically satisfying than a mixed vegetation of grasses, wild flowers and shrubs. Herbicides should therefore be used with due care and discrimination.

Areas kept close mown to lawn height often get infested with 'rosette' type weeds, the most common of which are plantains and daisy. As already suggested, improved management in the form of less severe cutting and the use of fertilisers is the only long-term solution to this problem. Plantains, however, and some other common weeds of lawns, such as creeping buttercup and hawkweed, are susceptible to the selective herbicides, MCPA and 24-D. Spraying with these chemicals could be used to eradicate such weeds in the first instance and improved management used to prevent their return. Daisy and other weeds frequently found in lawns, such as black medic, self heal, bulbous buttercup, celandine, pearlwort, chickweed, dandelion, white clover and the speedwells are more resistant to these chemicals so that mixtures of herbicides, including materials such as Mecoprop, Dichlorprop, Fenoprop or Dicamba, which control a broader spectrum of weeds, must be used. Even then, complete control of weeds may not be obtained with a single application.

Most weeds in grass which is allowed to grow to the hay stage are not objectionable provided they are looked upon as part of our heritage of wild flowers. Stinging nettles, however, can be a great nuisance—partly because they grow in dense clumps, to the exclusion of all other species, and partly because of the discomfort they can cause by stinging. MCPA and 24-D will kill the above-ground parts of nettles but regeneration from the roots is often rapid. Repeated sprayings with these chemicals are therefore necessary to 'wear down' and finally kill this weed. On isolated clumps Mecoprop or 2,4,5-T may be used and are generally more effective.

Certain woody species, such as gorse or the seedlings and saplings of ash, sycamore, alder, birch, hazel, hawthorn and elder, might

58

conceivably become a nuisance in churchyards. Possibly the best solution would be to allow them to develop so that the natural succession from rank grassland to deciduous forest would take its course. The process might be controlled to some extent by retaining the more valuable or interesting saplings and removing some or all of the others. Many woody species, however, can be controlled to a greater or lesser degree with the chemicals 234-T and ammonium sulphamate applied in various ways. A detailed study would be necessary in every situation to decide upon the best combination of chemical, dilutent and method of application.

Occasionally it may be desirable to kill all the existing vegetation of a piece of ground with herbicides. Several types are available, but since this is not a handbook on weed control they cannot all be discussed in detail. A general consideration is whether the intention is to keep the area clear of vegetation or whether subsequent re-seeding is envisaged. If the former, regular minimum follow-up dressings will be necessary to maintain a vegetation-free soil. If the latter, the type of herbicide, strength of solution and time of application will have to be carefully considered in relation to the timing of subsequent re-seeding and the type of vegetation envisaged as replacement flora.

Annual weeds and some weed grasses can be controlled in beds devoted to roses, and some other plants with the herbicides Paraquat and Dalapon. Weeds in gravel and other paths can be initially killed with appropriate herbicides then kept clear of germinating seedlings with persistent chemicals such as Atrazine and Simazine.

There is no doubt that really healthy looking green grass can only be the result of healthy growth. New young green shoots are being continuously produced to replace the older 'tatty' leaves. Grass which is suppressed by chemicals can only present old dark-coloured leaves. Generally therefore, unless it is impossible to avoid, mowing is to be preferred to the use of grass suppressants. If, however, a case for mummifying grass in any particular situation can be made, the chemical suppressant that should be used is maleic hydrazide.

SEEDING

Most churchyards are already covered with vegetation of one sort or another. The cases where complete re-seeding is required are likely to be rare. It is possible to envisage two likely situations. One is where an area is not immediately required and can therefore be passed over to a farmer for grazing or cutting. The other is where an area is cleared of kerbs and stones and is subsequently so uneven as to require levelling off and re-seeding. There may be others. In all cases there will be common problems of cultivation and management.

Grass and legume seeds are small, and if they are to germinate and establish well they must be sown in a fine firm seed bed. After the primary cultivation, such as ploughing or rotavating, repeated harrowing and rolling should be carried out so that soil particles become progressively finer and consolidated prior to sowing. After seeds are broadcast on to the surface of the soil, they must be harrowed in (*i.e.* covered with soil) and again rolled down firmly.

Seedlings can only establish quickly and well if they are provided with adequate plant foods. Acid soils should be limed after ploughing and a complete compound fertiliser worked into the seed bed during the final operations of harrowing and rolling.

If an area is to be handed over to a farmer for use, he should be given the opportunity of stipulating which seeds mixture he requires for the purpose to which the area is to be put. A different mixture will usually be required for grazing than for hay production, for instance. It should be sown at agricultural seed rates. A proportion of long-lived varieties of grasses should always be included since re-seeding is an expensive operation, and the less frequently it has to be repeated the better. For general purposes a mixture of varieties of perennial ryegrass (including a long-lived one as already indicated) with timothy and white clover is likely to be satisfactory.

For other areas in the churchyard proper, which would need to be cut purely as a maintenance operation, grasses which do not grow too tall or too fast would have obvious advantages. Generally, what are normally known as the 'fine' lawn grasses have these characteristics and also tend to make a springy, hard-wearing turf. A mixture of 70 per cent creeping red fescue and 30 per cent agrostis tenuis is a good general-purpose mixture, and if sown at half an ounce per square yard need not be prohibitively expensive. A small amount of wild white clover seed added to this mixture will help to keep the sward green and healthy, even during periods of drought, without altering its dwarf habit of growth.

CONSERVATION

The climax vegetation for most of Great Britain is deciduous forest. Grassland which is not grazed or cut becomes long and rank. This causes light to be excluded from the base of the plants and they tend to become separated by bare soil. The next stage is for the bare soil to be colonised by seedlings of small shrubs and scrub plants. Finally, saplings of trees become established and eventually provide a complete canopy so that the climax stage is reached. It would obviously not be desirable to have all churchyards revert to deciduous forest any more than it would be to have them all as well kept lawns. For most, some sort of compromise would be best. If the right degree of compromise can be achieved, work will be reduced and many interesting species of wild plants conserved.

Various compromises have already been suggested in the sections on degree and frequency of cutting of grass. Another approach would be to have no wholesale grass cutting but to allow the natural succession to take its course for a year or so. When shrubs and saplings of trees begin to appear, these should be treated on an individual basis. Common shrub plants, such as hawthorn, blackthorn and wart willow, could be thinned out and removed. Canopy-forming trees, especially those which cast a light shade, *e.g.* rowan, birch and sycamore of the shorter trees and oak or ash of the tall forest-making trees, could be encouraged simply by leaving them. Alternatively, it may be thought desirable to encourage trees which throw a dense shade such as beech or conifers. These have very little undergrowth so that the work of cutting it is reduced to a minimum. Please read Chapter 1 before deciding on the advisability of using herbicides.

MAINTENANCE OF STONE, BRICK AND FLINT WALLS AND PROTECTION OF WOODWORK

Pointing Many old church and churchyard walls were built of soft stone, or of mixed materials, intended to be protected by a plaster rendering. If this remains, it must be patched with lime plaster *not* cement plaster, and lime-washed, *not* distempered, every ten years or so. Pointing in an old wall must be done with lime mortar, *not* cement mortar, because scientists now know that strong cement is injurious to old stone, and that its use will soon make matters worse. The Society for the Protection of Ancient Buildings is accustomed to recommend the mortar described here, because it is known to be safe and to set well. Six or seven parts of coarse, clean sand to be mixed with one part of lime (ground, slaked or hydrated), beaten up with water at the same time. This may be left to stand, being kept moist. When it is wanted, it may be used in the following proportions; six or seven parts of the mixture to be knocked up with one part of ordinary Portland cement, the whole being thoroughly incorporated. The proportion of cement used may be reduced, but in general this makes a reliable mortar of an agreeable colour and texture for use on old stone and brickwork. The joints should be flush with the stone and given a rubbed or brushed finish.

Preserving wooden gates, fences and sheds   Timber used out of doors in its natural state will deteriorate sooner or later by weathering and decay. Weathering, which is caused by the combined action of sunlight, rain and oxidation, quickly destroys the natural colour of wood, turning it grey. It also gradually roughens and erodes the surface, but the action is extremely slow and not important from the strength aspect. Fungal decay is the main hazard of external timbers, causing most of the damage that occurs in practice. Insect attack also occurs in exterior woodwork but usually only in wood which is already decaying.

Timber will rot only if it is damp, and when used under permanently damp conditions, *e.g.* in direct contact with the earth, many woods such as beech, birch and spruce are destroyed rapidly. Others, however, are sufficiently durable to last for a long time under such conditions, for example 4 by 4 inch (102 by 102 mm) oak heartwood posts will give good service for forty years or more without any preservative treatment. Under less severe conditions of exposure, *e.g.* weatherboarding, gates, fencing boards and rails, decay is generally slower and there are a number of other common woods, in addition to oak, such as larch, western red cedar and African mahogany, which will last well without preservation. However, it is worthwhile applying some form of preservative treatment to all timber outside so that the maximum life is obtained, with consequent savings in maintenance and repairs.

The most effective treatment for new timber is pressure-impregnation with creosote or a water-borne preservative, and timber so treated can be obtained from firms distributed throughout the country. Pressure-treatment should always be used for timber in direct contact with the ground, and is preferable in other situations especially when timbers of low natural durability are employed. If the treated wood is to be painted afterwards, then a water-borne preservative and not creosote must be employed. The use of pressure-treated material, however, is not always practicable, especially when only small quantities of wood are involved or general maintenance and repairs are done on a 'do-it-yourself' basis. In these circumstances, simpler methods of treatment such as brushing and dipping must be used. These are not as effective as pressure-impregnation and treatment must be repeated regularly to preserve the timber over a long period. When applying a wood preservative by brush the liquid should be flooded over the wood and care taken that all joints, cracks and end-grain receive a liberal application, as it is in such places that decay usually starts. Two or three coats can be given, with a few days interval between each. The surface of the wood should be clean and dry. On the average, one gallon of preservative will cover about 300 square feet (27·9 sq m) of surface. Somewhat better treatment is obtained if the wood is immersed in a tank of preservative. A minimum dipping time of ten minutes should be given, but if the wood can be left to soak for a longer period, even for several days, then much better results are obtained. If it is not possible to obtain a tank big enough to take the timber, then the ends of the planks or posts can be immersed in turn in a bucket of preservative and left to soak for a time, the sides of the timber being given a brush treatment. Any of the modern tar oil and organic solvent preservatives are satisfactory for external woodwork, and where their colour and odour do not matter, one of the dipping grades of creosote would be a cheap and effective preservative to use. Sometimes, when it is desired that the natural appearance of the timber is retained, then a clear water-repellent preservative or a mixture of linseed oil (1 part) and a colourless preservative (2 parts) should be used. When timber is treated initially by brushing or dipping, it is necessary to renew the treatment every few years or so by brushing on more preservative.

In general, the treatment of old timbers *in situ* must be carried out by brushing. This should be done in warm weather when the surface of the wood is dry. The preservative should be applied liberally, as for new timber, and one gallon will cover about 100 square feet (9·35 sq m) of surface. For general purposes, creosote is satisfactory, but for old and valuable woodwork where appearance is important and protection from weathering is desirable, then a clear water-repellent preservative should be used. Timber that is carved, for example, should be treated with this type of preservative to protect the surface from weathering. Posts should have the earth dug away around them to a depth of about 12 inches (305 mm) so that the most vulnerable part is accessible for treatment. Decayed wood and dirt should be scraped off the post, after which it should receive a heavy application of preservative. If the wood is very wet, a water-borne preservative should be used, but otherwise creosote is satisfactory. A good treatment for large posts and posts forming part of important structures is to wrap a preservative bandage around them before replacing the soil. Western red cedar shingles, which may be used for lych-gate roofs, should be brush or spray treated every few years or so, and it is advisable also to treat new shingles either by brushing or by dipping the bundles of shingles in a wood preservative, before laying them.

The names of suppliers of pressure-treated timber and preservative bandages, and information on the various types of proprietary wood preservatives, can be obtained from the British Wood Preserving Association, 6 Southampton Place, London, W.C.I.

11. *Alterations to the churchyard*

Gravestones, kerbs and mounds are sometimes regarded as obstacles to the easy maintenance of the grass. Any proposals put forward for their removal or re-arrangement require careful scrutiny and must never detract from the essential character of a churchyard as the place of burial near a church. This character, as we have said elsewhere, is not best maintained by treating the churchyard as though it were a garden or a park. At the earliest stage the parish (or in some cases it may be the local authority) should consult the church architect and the Diocesan Advisory Committee for advice on what tombstones should in any event be retained *in situ*. The presumption should be, in fact, that most of them will be retained—kerbstones and, to a lesser degree, mounds are in a different category. It may also be necessary to arrange for the lifting and refixing of sunken gravestones, so that they will be more visible and less of a hazard. Table tombs may require repointing or other repair.

Any scheme which involves the removal or substantial repair of stones or kerbs or mounds is a matter for an application for faculty. The value of this statutory protection is particularly apparent in such a situation. It allows a parish some freedom of action while at the same time enabling interested parties to state their case; and it inhibits the wholesale or thoughtless destruction of valuable historical evidence.

Generally speaking there will be no objection to the removal of kerbs or mounds completely, or totally illegible and irreparably damaged stones. It should be remembered, though, that what will appear illegible to most people will not necessarily be illegible to the expert—and the recording of gravestones and their inscriptions demands expert attention. Kerbs may be sunk or laid level with the turf or preferably removed altogether. If there are inscriptions on the kerb the face can be turned so that the words are still readable. The simplest method is to dig a trench alongside and turn the kerb into its own 'grave'. Mounds must be treated with respect; they were once the marker for the poor man's grave. Therefore it is all the more impor-tant that specific mention is included in the faculty application. If permission is given for their removal, mounds can best be levelled by a

65

straight incision up the centre and the earth removed from under the turf. Alternatively soil from other graves can be put alongside to build up the level. Prevention is better than cure and in filling a new grave not all the excavated earth on top of the grave need be replaced. The majority of illegible stones or seriously damaged stones can be removed altogether; but care should be taken when any are of aesthetic, historical or genealogical value. They may also be protecting other and exceptionally interesting gravestones from severe weathering. Certain wrought-iron railings and chains are also of value and advice should be sought before considering their removal.

Any scheme for the re-arrangement of gravestones will depend upon the purpose of the exercise. In all cases where the churchyard forms a setting for the church the preservation of the churchyard's character as a church burial ground should be kept in mind, and many if not all the older stones should be preserved *in situ*. If the primary purpose is to release an area of the churchyard for reburial then some stones can be re-aligned or their position altered to enable new graves to be dug. Such a scheme means that an area need not be cleared all at once but can be prepared as the space is required. In that case particular thought needs to be given to the type and material of the new monuments which should be permitted amongst the older stones.

If the scheme is primarily to make it easier to use mechanical implements for regular maintenance work then the re-arrangement must be planned to permit their easy use and manœuvring. The scale of a churchyard normally requires the mechanical implement to be guided by a man on foot: a tractor will in most cases be over-large and inappropriate.

Sometimes the drawing up of a scheme is taken as the opportunity for weeding out some of the more glaring and inharmonious tombstones such as those made of white marble or black granite in a churchyard where natural stone of sympathetic colour is otherwise extensively used. At the same time less aesthetically satisfying designs (*e.g.* birdbaths and the like) could be moved to some less obtrusive part of the churchyard. Generally, tombstones which are moved for the sake of easier maintenance should be reinstated as near as possible to their original positions.

The Commonwealth War Graves Commission has had experience of headstones being removed from Commonwealth war graves without any prior notification to the Commission. This is unfortunate, and it is most important to ensure that if any tentative proposals are envisaged which involve Commonwealth war graves or headstones the Commission should be informed at once through the Diocesan Registrar. Headstones which are the responsibility of the Commission are not necessarily of the standard type and may not therefore be readily recognisable, and it is therefore advisable that the Commission should be notified as a matter of courtesy in all cases where a faculty application involves removal of headstones.

The simplest re-arrangement of stones is to re-arrange them in parallel rows, but this is totally to destroy the churchyard pattern. Where a larger area of cut grass is required tombstones could be arranged in short lines parallel to the churchyard wall and set in gravel so that weeds can be easily contained. Sometimes the number of stones might suggest the placing of them back to back. The general rule is that the minimum number of stones should be moved from their original position. But unless as in parts of Lancashire or Yorkshire (*e.g.* the churchyards of St John and St Peter in the heart of Leeds) there is a local tradition in the placing of gravestones level with the ground, the effect of producing a virtually paved area and the removal of every vertical scale in a churchyard can be disastrous. Tombstones should never be laid beside or stacked against a churchyard wall like a pack of cards. If you are unfortunate to have inherited a churchyard where this has happened, consideration should be given to restoring them to their rightful place.

Only completely decayed stones should be broken up and buried in the churchyard. The greatest scandal can be, and regrettably has been, caused by the sale of such stones or by deliberate defacement or damage. Do not 'mark' memorials with any type of paint.

SUGGESTED PROCEDURE

Each churchyard is individual and demands individual treatment. In addition to seeking advice from outside the parish, *e.g.* from the Diocesan Advisory Committee and the inspecting architect, the congregation should itself be asked for ideas and suggestions. Someone from the Diocesan Advisory Committee or the local history society, might be asked to take parishioners on a 'churchyard walk' pointing out the different styles, the meaning of the symbolism, and the historical content of the inscriptions. Interest may be aroused in local schools, leading to the school-children making a survey of the churchyard, and producing a report on their findings. Oxford University Press have published a pamphlet on this subject for use in schools in their *Schools Council Integrated Studies* series.

No action should be taken until all ideas have been considered and the best solution for your particular churchyard decided upon. You may indeed find that no change is the best solution. What is right for a neighbouring churchyard will almost entirely not be right for yours—although it is useful to see what has been done elsewhere, even if only to see how not to do it. The test is both to ensure that nothing is destroyed which ought to be preserved and that the setting of the church should still be appropriate. In the *Herefordshire* volume in the Buildings of England series, Sir Nikolaus Pevsner pinpoints exactly what ought not to happen in the case of one important church (Leominster Priory):

> 'The church today stands, pale red on juicy green, in a curious isolation surrounded on three sides by lawn (at the churchyard), and these lawns and open spaces stretch quite a distance to the south. The building looks thus neither like a priory church nor like a parish church. One is almost reminded of a model.'

To sum up, all monuments or fragments earlier than the early nineteenth century should be kept, virtually without exception. Every churchyard monument of the seventeenth and eighteenth centuries is likely to be of good design and craftsmanship, and equally will be of genealogical interest to historians and demographers. Tombstones of this period should only be destroyed if past all repair. Nineteenth-century monuments may also be worth preserving both for intrinsic merit and for genealogical or historical interest. If the churchyard is overcrowded, untidy and difficult to mow some modest degree of partial clearance may be desirable, but it is unnecessary elements like kerbs, bird-baths and vases which should be reviewed first; then, if still more room for manœuvre is required, stones which have become featureless or illegible or broken beyond repair might be considered. The object should be to obtain enough leeway in which to use a mower and to free the walls of the church from obstructions, not to release space for ambitious gardening. *Every effort should be made not to change radically the appearance and character of the churchyard.*

The recommended procedure is as follows:

1. To prepare a numbered plan and a register of graves with a copy in full of each monumental inscription. The recording of the inscrip-

tions should be carried out by someone with a proper interest and the necessary expertise. Recording the appearance of gravestones and their carvings and inscriptions by means of photographs and drawings is also desirable.

2. To consult the Diocesan Advisory Committee who will advise upon monuments of outstanding merit that ought to be preserved. A delegation or representative of the DAC will usually make a visit of inspection before the advice can be given.

3. After consultation with the DAC (and, if so advised, with the inspecting architect) to list the tombstones which it is desired to clear and to decide, again with the advice of the DAC, what to do with them.

4. To apply for a faculty, when the Registrar will advise what should be done about consulting the relatives or representatives of any persons whose tombstones are to be displaced, if they are of recent date.

5. Subject to the advice of the Registrar, to advertise the proposal in the local press, inviting objectors, if any, to come forward by a certain date. (This is a legal requirement, but in fact it is still more desirable that any proposal involving alterations to a churchyard should be the subject of a sympathetic and informative article in the local newspaper which will explain to the interested public at large what is intended.)

12. Recording the churchyard

The importance of keeping a record of all burials in a churchyard in current use cannot be too strongly emphasised. The distress, expense and notoriety consequent upon interment in the wrong grave should be sufficient incentive for a proper map and list of stones and graves to be kept. Of equal importance, however, is the recording of gravestones in a churchyard or part of a churchyard which is no longer in use. In particular, where gravestones are to be removed or their position altered, we hope that applicants for the necessary faculty required for this work will be ordered to provide some survey as a record comparable to what is outlined below.

The recording of a churchyard involves the fully surveyed plan of the churchyard, boundaries, paths and graves on a scale large enough for the location of any gravestones to be related to the grave beneath with a maximum error of one foot or 300 mm each way. A rudimentary plan can be drawn up using a sheet of squared paper. A large scale O.S. map can be enlarged to provide the outlines of the church walls, churchyard boundaries and paths. Some significant point in the churchyard—a large monument, crossed paths or such like should then be accurately plotted and the graves marked in relation to it. Each row should be lettered and the individual grave given a letter. In the older parts of some churchyards the graves are not always in exact rows and care must be taken to allow for the odd grave which has slipped a row. A book or card-index should be kept to record the inscription, style and material of the stone and other relevant details. For an example of one index card see the example used at Penn Churchyard, Bucks, Appendix VI(a).

With regard to a fuller and more detailed survey the services of a photographer will be required; and though there may not be a surveyor in the parish there will undoubtedly be several keen amateur photographers. The Council of British Archaeology and Rescue have produced a paper, *How to Record a Churchyard*, Jeremy Jones (CBA/Rescue 1975) and we are indebted to the author and publisher for the following brief summary of what is recommended:

The usual procedure is to number each stone with a temporary label affixed to an inconspicuous part of the stone, and make a plan at a scale of 1:250. The outline of the churchyard can be based on that in the 1:2500 inch O.S. map. The stones are then photographed with a scale, larger numbers being put on the stone while the photograph is being taken so that the stone number and photograph can easily be correlated. A good photographer using a 35 mm SLR camera can utilise natural or artificial light to show as much detail as possible, preferably with the light sources coming from the top left. The photographic forms are made to a size of 90 by 90 mm to fit the specification recording forms. [For a specimen form see Appendix VI(b).]

The photograph is the primary record and should be made before the form is filled in; it will be found that if the photograph is good much written description (for example of the shape and decoration) can be omitted; it will also act as a check on the transcription of the lettering.

The time taken to record a churchyard depends on many factors, such as the number of stones, the amount of clearance that has to be done before the survey can be undertaken, how much individual stones are obscured, the legibility of the inscriptions and so forth. Where the recording is of no urgency, the work may continue systematically for several months. In cases of urgency some record can be made in a short time. As an experiment at a Birmingham University residential course, ten students recorded 200 stones in Wroxeter churchyard in three days; this included a plan, photographs and forms.

The cost of the survey will include that of duplicating or buying the forms and final typing of the data sheets—perhaps 30p per stone (at 1975 prices), a small price to pay for the recording of a unique memorial.

The record, of course, is the important thing; once this is completed anyone can analyse the data at any time; it may be the recorder will do this as part of a study of the parish history; or the dates may be used by regional or national studies by a professional researcher on the subject.

When a survey is completed one set of records (plan, forms and photographs) should be deposited in the church safe, one in the County Record Office and a third in the local library or with the local Archaeological Society.

13. Lych-gates

The entrance to many churchyards is through some form of lych-gate. These gates are often thought of as ornamental archways but in fact they take many forms, and are strictly functional in origin. Their purpose is to shelter the coffin and the bearers when a funeral procession pauses to await the priest coming out from the church to meet them.

In some places the centre of the gateway is occupied by a lych-stone, on which the body rested. In the western counties this may lie between two passage ways or Cornish stiles with a seat on either side, but without any super-structure. Sometimes a wicket-gate may be provided at the side for use when the central passage is not required, and there must be many places where the lych-stone or a wooden central coffin rest has been removed in later times to allow a wheeled bier to pass through.

Lych-gates were in some districts built wholly of wood; in others, of wood on a stone base; but elsewhere entirely of stone. A few here and there are combined with a clerk's or sexton's cottage to form a gate house.

Ancient lych-gates were not very high, nor had they the ambitious scale or detail often seen in nineteenth century and more recent versions. They were directly functional, and depended for their beauty on simplicity, proportion and good craftsmanship, never seeming to be in architectural competition with the church itself. Good Victorian architects saw the lych-gate as an integral part of the wall surrounding the churchyard; and the inter-relationship between them (and also between lych-gate, wall and the church itself) is often of considerable aesthetic importance (*see* Fig 19).

In designing a new gate, consideration should be given to its function. It should be made of sufficient depth—at least 7 feet (2·134 m) and of sufficient width to accommodate the bearers. The height is also of importance if vehicles are to pass through. In materials it should follow local tradition, being made of stone in a stone district and wood or brick where these prevail, with a roof covering to harmonise with the church. In design it is reasonable to look for ancient precedents, but this need not entail a recreation of the past. What is important is a

FIG. 19 Coalpit Heath, Gloucestershire: the lych-gate designed by William Butterfield, 1844–5. In this instance the lych-gate is of major significance in the architect's work, being described by Henry-Russell Hitchcock as follows: 'Only the stone lych-gate, with its simple forms and curious juxtaposition of angles, suggests the pungent sort of originality Butterfield's finest work was to display later.'

[*Photograph*: National Monuments Record]

To face page 72

FIG. 20 The cross which is a notable feature of the churchyard extension at Penn, Buckinghamshire. See also the text note on this in Chapter 15.

[*Photograph: Darsie Rawlins*]

FIG. 21   The town centre churchyard at Banbury showing the effect achieved by a landscape architect. See also text note in Chapter 18.

[*Photographs:* Paul and Sarah Gosling]

FIG. 22   A Book of Remembrance for St Martin le Grand, Coney Street, York, designed by the late George G. Pace. See also text note on p. 100.

[*Photograph:* Kershaw Studios]

respect for local traditions and for context. In any event a faculty will be needed and the Diocesan Advisory Committee should be consulted. In many country parishes, a well-placed tree near the church gate is as effective as a lych-gate.

In making provision for access for invalids it is not desirable to place concrete ramps over the steps into the churchyard; an alternative entrance is the best solution.

In repairing ancient lych-gates, care should be taken to preserve all original material and to follow the techniques of the original builders. This is specialist work, which needs to be supervised by a sensitive architect. Many lych-gates are spoiled by straightforward neglect. Lamps need replacing or repairing from time to time. Advice on preservative treatment for old wood, and on the pointing of brick and stone, is given in Chapter 10. Readers wishing to learn more about old lych-gates in their various forms are referred to the standard work on the subject, now more than half a century old, Aymer Vallance's *Old Crosses & Lychgates* (Batsford, 1920).

14. *Walls, fences, hedges and gates*

The form taken by the churchyard boundary enclosure naturally varies with the site and with local materials and building traditions. Its principal purpose in the country will be to prevent the straying of stock; in the town, the trespass of passers by, the treading of short cuts and the accumulation of litter.

In a village, when on one side the street and on the other houses and gardens abut on the churchyard, the boundary is usually a fairly substantial wall; but where the churchyard is surrounded by fields, it is often only a hedge. Such walls or hedges demand careful and skilled maintenance. The walls may be of very considerable age. Even if only a century old, they are often of aesthetic importance. Having been more or less utilitarian in origin they have become mellowed in appearance. Victorian architects took great care to relate the design and texture of the churchyard wall to the church itself.

Some walls may be found of medieval date and of considerable antiquarian value. They frequently incorporate older stones including fragments of memorials and are sometimes finished with a well-proportioned stone coping which may prove to have been re-used from an earlier building. Many churchyard walls are of a composite structure, having been rebuilt piecemeal in a variety of materials and techniques at different times, and incorporating portions of really early work. (One churchyard had as many as fifty-five householders each responsible for a section of the boundary.) All these old walls, however irregular and patchy, should be carefully preserved and no alteration made except after investigation by the Diocesan Advisory Committee. They should be particularly examined to see if names or initials of past parishioners, once responsible for maintaining parts of the boundary survive—examples exist at Cowfold, Sussex and Church Stretton, Salop.

In Wiltshire and the adjacent parts of Berkshire, Hampshire and Dorset, the older boundary walls are often of cob and are sometimes finished with a covering of thatch like a miniature roof—a necessary protection which, with the thick limewash to preserve the face of the cob itself from water penetration, should be periodically renewed.

As with the walls of the church itself, care should be taken with the pointing. Ivy and other plants should not be allowed to grow on churchyard walls on account of their destructive character. Appendix IV gives advice on how to deal with such plants.

Continuous reburial in the same area has often caused the churchyard earth level to rise above that of the road outside. The consequent pressure causes the wall to bulge. Perimeter trees may also present a similar problem. Rebuilding the wall can be expensive. In a Closed Churchyard repair is the local authority's responsibility; in one which has not been closed by an Order in Council, help may also be obtained (*see* Chapter 25).

Wooden fences, where traditional, should be renewed with a similar form of construction. They should be treated regularly with creosote to preserve them—preferably the timber for a new fence should be pressure-impregnated before delivery.

Some wrought-iron and most cast-iron railings are old and valuable; there are many good eighteenth-century examples in towns, and both early and later nineteenth-century work is now coming to be properly appreciated. London has some notable examples of all periods, especially in the churchyards of St Paul's Cathedral and St Martin-in-the-Fields. Good iron gates are fairly common and usually attractive; they should be preserved by regular painting. Valuable iron work which has perished through rust and neglect can be re-annealed.

In certain cases iron railings of inferior design may be replaced by a simple stone, brick or wood boundary wall or fence. Sometimes the appearance of a building is spoiled by surrounding it with railings; much worse, however, are concrete posts and wire netting. If ever fences or railings have to be designed to be so high that they are virtually unclimbable, or made from very cheap utilitarian materials, they can to some extent be improved in appearance by providing brick or stone gate posts, and piers carefully designed and placed at intervals.

All new work should generally be simple; obtrusively ornamental walling is always a mistake. As with the wall or fence, so with gates. In the country it is usually better to avoid iron, and to make a good solid wooden gate following the lines of local craft tradition. In a town and in districts where the use of iron has long been traditional it remains the obvious choice. Opportunity should then be found to provide a really distinguished design or perhaps re-use gates of fine quality. Never buy such things, whether small or large, from a catalogue: they need designing to fit into the site. Good work can be provided often by the local blacksmiths and craftsmen listed by the Council for Small Industries in Rural Areas (CoSIRA). The design must always be supervised by the church architect, the Diocesan Advisory Committee should be consulted, and a faculty sought.

If the gates are of wood, the side which is not generally in use should be bolted to the ground to relieve the weight on the hinges.

In some districts a churchyard stile is found. These are often old and always picturesque, even if sometimes inconvenient. They usually follow the distinctive traditional form for stiles in the part of the country they are in, and thus possess a strong local flavour and interest; this should be carefully maintained and preserved.

Hedges should receive the skilled attention of a first-class hedger from time to time. Unless they are properly cut and laid periodically, they will get thin at the bottom, or spread out and waste ground. If local farmers cannot supply skilled labour the Inspectorate of the Ministry of Agriculture can advise. For the encouragement of wild life, the best type of hedge is A-shaped, thick at the bottom and narrow at the top with a few feet of uncut grassland at the foot. The nesting season should be avoided for hedging *i.e.* April to early July.

15. Churchyard crosses

ANCIENT CROSSES

The churchyard cross often preceded the erection of a church building. In very early times, when these buildings were scarcely distinguishable from secular ones, such a symbol was essential.

The cross was the predominant feature in every churchyard before the Reformation. In districts where good stone is abundant, medieval survivals—often fragmentary—are common. On either side of the Bristol Channel, and also in many parts of the Midlands, there is scarcely a churchyard which does not have some considerable fragments. Occasionally, as at Chewton Mendip and Stringston in Somerset, and at St Donats and Llangan in the Vale of Glamorgan, the cross is complete; so also are many of the earlier crosses in Cornwall. In eastern and south-eastern England, however, remains of churchyard crosses are exceptional. We know from documents that they existed, but they must often have been of wood and therefore easily destroyed by the Puritans or by the elements and, in later times, perhaps removed to make room for graves.

All remains of churchyard crosses should, of course, be faithfully recorded and preserved. It is long since any such relics were wilfully destroyed but there have been some injurious, although well-intentioned, restorations of ancient crosses. Heads and shafts of purely conjectural, if not actually misleading, type have been added to old bases, and these have often been too heavily repaired in order to support the new work. Here and there an original head has been recovered and replaced. This is generally the right course, but opportunities of doing it are not likely to occur very frequently. The fixing of a new head to an ancient shaft is not without practical as well as aesthetic risks as the ancient stone may split on the insertion of dowels or, as a result of the increased weight, through wind resistance and leverage.

As a general rule, remains of churchyard crosses should be no more than cleaned and conserved, and not restored by the addition of new work. Even this treatment requires specialist advice. Where the steps are loose or sundered by vegetation they may need to be reset, care being taken to use the proper method of pointing. If they have sunk

77

into the ground, they can be prised up and reset on a concrete base. Such an exercise may provide an opportunity for archaeological investigation.

MODERN CROSSES

Where remains of an old cross exist, and it is desired to erect a new one, an entirely different design should preferably be chosen. By ancient tradition the cross was generally near the principal entrance to the church. Where no traces of an old cross survive, the new one may be placed nearby but, where remains of an old cross exist, the new one should be placed elsewhere. Indeed it may be preferable to set up the new cross in a dominating position in an extension of the churchyard. The churchyard extension at Penn, Buckinghamshire is shown in Figure 20 in relation to the church itself. The late Sir Edwin Maufe, who designed the new churchyard extension, retained the eighteenth century red brick former garden walls to give a sense of enclosure and placed his formal layout within the space so enclosed. Conspicuously placed at the junction of the main axes is the cross, carved by the sculptor Darsie Rawlins who lives locally. On one side is the Holy Spirit in the form of a dove, and on the other (see detail photograph) is carved the Blessed Virgin and the Holy Child; a choice of iconography which is both unusual and, in this context, moving. In any case, the cross should not be too near the building. Wherever it is placed, it should always face towards the west, like the rood or the altar cross within the church. The adoption of this common-sense rule, always observed of old, does much to secure an appearance of congruity with the church building.

Special care should be taken that a modern cross, especially if it is adjoining an ancient church, is neither too large nor too elaborate. The Diocesan Advisory Committee should always be consulted about the design and situation of a new cross or the repair of an old one.

16. Drainage

The drainage of the churchyard itself is vital to the maintenance of the church building only in cases where the flooding of boiler houses or burial vaults is experienced or where the church obstructs the natural disposal of surface water from a steeply sloping site; more important is adequate provision for the drainage of rainwater discharged from the roofs. Disposal may be by gutters and downpipes, from overhanging eaves or by means of projecting rainwater spouts. In the first method it is essential that the concentrated rainwater discharge should be quickly and effectively dispersed through surface channels or gullies and underground drainpipes to soakaways or ditches. Where roofs drain by means of overhanging eaves a perimeter channel linked to underground drains or, alternatively, a subsoil with good drainage properties is essential if the wall footings are not to become saturated. Where spouts are used, carefully sited catchment areas, again linked to underground drains, are necessary where the absorption quality of the subsoil is poor.

As historic churches were constructed without damp-proof courses they are invariably by modern standards damp and, where the wall core is of loosely constituted rubble of some thickness, poorly suited to proprietary damp-proofing techniques. This is not necessarily the disadvantage it was once supposed provided the interior wall finishes, panelling and floor surfaces are designed to perform in above-average moisture conditions and to facilitate the evaporation of dampness absorbed from the soil outside.

Unnecessary damage is on occasion caused by the construction of drain trenches at wall bases where the ground level of the churchyard is higher than that of the floor within. Such trenches can undermine the shallow wall footings of medieval buildings, expose the supporting subsoil to frost attack, and destroy important archaeological material. Provided gutters, downpipes, gullies and drains are not leaking or blocked (nine out of ten cases of severe damp damage are due to gutter and gully defects) it is generally possible to keep rising damp at an acceptable level without recourse to exterior trenching.

In cases where an existing ground drainage system is functioning

79

imperfectly or has become blocked, cleaning and repairs should always be attempted initially. Where repairs are not possible expert advice should automatically be sought before radical changes are enacted. Drainage improvements, in common with all alterations to church buildings, require faculty consent, as does any disturbance of human remains which frequently lie buried at shallow levels in unmarked positions beneath the surface of the churchyard.

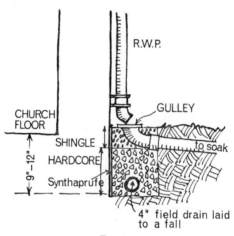

FIG. 23

Fig 23 shows the construction of a 'French' drain, which can *sometimes* be an appropriate solution for damp church walls. In addition to the structural problems which need to be taken into account (see previous page) this is also the most sensitive area archaeologically and special care needs to be taken when such a drain is laid.

Prevention, however, is better than cure. Walk round the church each week to ensure that gullies and channels are clear of dead leaves. Watch for flooding and blocked drains after heavy rain. Lift manhole covers and rod drains annually. Make a map of the drains surrounding the church and hang a copy in the vestry. Fasten another in the front of the fabric maintenance log-book. Vigilance costs nothing and can literally save money being poured down the drain.

17. Paths

Much of the beauty and seemliness of a churchyard depends on its paths.

A clear distinction can be made between paths to the main church doors and those surrounding the church or leading to a side entrance. The main path should be wide enough for a coffin to be carried comfortably—5 to 6 feet (1·5 to 1·8 m) is a fair width—and side fencing should be avoided. If the path is too narrow, people are encouraged to walk on the grass. It is often economically impossible to surface side paths but these can sometimes be left and kept regularly mown.

While old paving should be scrupulously retained, the main approaches must be kept in safe condition for pedestrians. A hard gravel path is traditional in some districts; in others, flat stones or bricks are used, sometimes with a border of another material such as cobble-stones or flints. A good deal of paving of this type is very old; it is important that local traditions of path-making or paving should be retained. Ornamental tiled edges are out of place, unless traditional. Weeds in gravel paths can be destroyed by Prefix granules or by watering with a solution of sodium chlorate in the proportion of 4 oz to 1 gallon (110 grams to 4·5 litres) of water. Algae can be removed from stone flags by an application of a very weak solution of 'Domestos'. Care must be taken as this solution will burn grass. Weeds in brick and stone-paved paths are most easily destroyed with a flame-gun.

When repaving or relaying churchyard paths, a careful watch should be kept for interesting and valuable monumental slabs, turned out of the church, and used either as paving or foundations of paths. The *mensa* of a pre-Reformation altar or the indented slabs of memorial brasses are not uncommon finds.

Parochial church councils should be urged to make a path all round but not too close to the church. It is important to be able to walk round the building in all weathers, as neglect and untidiness, unsightly sheds and rubbish heaps are most usual where they are not readily seen. Moreover, stopped gutters and gullies, and signs of decay will be more readily observed if perambulation does not entail wet feet.

Ashes, clinkers, and smooth tiles should not be used to make paths in churchyards, but in brick country ordinary walling bricks are often satisfactory. Concrete is satisfactory if roughly mixed.

Paths should not be excessively cambered; examples exist, unfortunately, in beautiful old churchyards where the paths have been relaid on a steep camber with concrete scored with a trowel to imitate crazy-paving.

In towns, where cost may be a first consideration, and there is no better material available, tarmac with a flush border of slabs or bricks may be used, but road metal macadam or gravel, well rolled, is to be preferred, as it dries quickly after rain. Tarmac in a country churchyard rarely looks well but its blackness can be tempered if gravel is rolled into it as a top dressing.

18. Shrubs and flowers

The crucial factor in considering the planting of shrubs and flowers in a churchyard is whether there is adequate, or indeed any, labour available for cultivation. If there is not, then grass alone should be allowed to grow and every effort made to keep it reasonably mown and trimmed. Few sights are more peaceful than a churchyard with well tended grass and clean, stone-paved, gravel, brick or cobbled paths.

If, however, labour is certain to be continually available for a foreseeable period of time, then the planting of a few shrubs might be considered. A useful guide is *Hillier's Manual of Trees and Shrubs*, available in either paperback or hard cover. In making a choice of shrubs, regard must be had to the climatic and local conditions, and obviously it is well worth while, in the first instance, consulting a reputable nurseryman, if possible a local grower.

Consideration must be given to the height (actual and potential) and to the root growth of both trees and shrubs and *nothing* should be planted in the vicinity of the church building, or close to any boundary walls where damage to the foundations may result from root growth and gutters are only too likely to become blocked by falling leaves and debris. Where a church stands back some distance from the road, evergreen shrubs flanking the path to the porch can offer some protection to worshippers from wind, rain and snow in addition to looking attractive. Ivy and other varieties of creeping plants should be banished from the immediate vicinity of the church—since, although picturesque in appearance, they will certainly cause harm to the building.

In previous editions of the *Handbook* it was urged that, where the atmosphere is heavy and polluted, evergreen shrubs should be avoided. This advice is still sound but, since the Clean Air Act came into being, there has been a consequent improvement in the urban atmosphere and in recent years it has become possible to be more adventurous again in the use of evergreen shrubs.

As to flowers, roses probably give the best value as they have a long flowering season. Rose bushes need pruning in early Spring, but this should present no difficulty to the amateur gardener. The most important point to consider is whether roses will really look suitable in the churchyard in question: in a country churchyard they will probably look out of place, perhaps less so in the suburbs or a town churchyard. Avoid too many of them, in any case. Remember also that roses grow old and need replacement. Bedding plants require regular attention, and this is certainly a reason for discouraging them. The majority of perennials, in particular, need constant staking and tying during the summer and in the autumn the plants must be cut down and divided where necessary. The making and keeping of a beautiful herbaceous border requires knowledge, skill and much patient work. By contrast a simple bed massed with an annual suitable to the locality can provide pleasing colour with much less work.

Colour can always be brought into a churchyard by planting bulbs, but it should be remembered that they will not grow successfully unless the grass is mown. Daffodils need planting informally by scattering and then digging them in where they fall. Wild daffodils, snowdrops and bluebells have the advantage that they can be massed in rough grass, however, and cyclamen thrive round the boles of certain trees—*Cyclamen europeum* flowering in spring and *C. hederifolium* in autumn. Clearly any decision to plant bulbs, as with anything else, will be governed by local conditions of soil and climate. In suitable soils, primroses are splendid; and, mercifully, they require no attention.

There are today a number of efficient weedkillers available and, if tempted to use them, it is vital to understand their range and intention. There are completely non-selective weedkillers, likely to destroy everything that comes into contact with them; avoid them. There are also selective kinds which, in varying degrees, kill off broad-leaved weeds but leave grass alone. In addition to these there are chemical retardants that inhibit the growth of grass (*see* Chapter 10). Some selective weedkillers can be used in well-established borders, but it is as well to study the instructions and obtain advice before applying a weedkiller.

If seats are provided in the churchyard, they should preferably be placed in a sheltered position, and in a town churchyard some attempt should be made to create a small local environment round them. Dame Sylvia Crowe is one of our most distinguished living landscape architects and it is a happy chance that at Banbury, Oxfordshire and also at Knaresborough in Yorkshire she has been commissioned to undertake work in the parish churchyards. At Knaresborough it will be some time before the ambitious scheme of planting is sufficiently mature to create the intended effect which is planned on an ample scale. At Banbury it is admirable what has been achieved by judicious thinning of stones, sensitive planting, and the provision of attractive, well-designed seating (*see* Fig 21). The guiding principle (as frequently expressed elsewhere in this *Handbook*) is that, whatever is undertaken to beautify the churchyard, the aim should be to maintain its essential character and not to create something like a public park.

Even if a churchyard is entirely disused and responsibility for its care transferred to the local authority under the *Open Spaces Act 1960*, it is still necessary for a faculty to be obtained for any proposed alterations. It is, of course, axiomatic that, where the churchyard remains the responsibility of the parish, whether or not it is closed for burials, any alteration to its layout, including flower beds, paved areas, new paths and so on, requires the sanction of a faculty just as much as the erection of a tombstone. This is an important safeguard of the rights of the parishioners, enabling them to object if any unwelcome or inappropriate change in the overall character of a churchyard is proposed.

19. Trees

Trees are important features in a churchyard. Often it would be difficult to imagine a particular church without its familar background or foreground of trees. Though frequently taken for granted, it is important to realise that they are living organisms which grow, flourish, decay and die and in due course have to be removed. The trees seen in churchyards today were planted by previous generations. It is the duty of each generation not only to safeguard them but to plan and plant for the future. In many instances well-loved trees have to be felled because they have become old and dangerous and it is then realised (too late) that this should have been foreseen and their successors planted a generation ago.

It is worth looking at and listing all the trees in the churchyard and considering each one of them in the light of both the present and the future.

THE PRESENT

Are there enough trees? Are there too many? Are any of them becoming dangerous, or throwing too much shade, or causing damp, or damaging walls, buildings or memorials? Should any be removed or lopped? Certain trees may have been listed and protected by the local authority by means of a Tree Preservation Order (TPO) and it is essential to be aware which trees are so protected.

THE FUTURE

What will each tree look like in twenty years' time, in fifty, in a hundred? Will it have died, or will it have been removed? Should new trees be planted now, or in ten years' time, to replace existing trees which will disappear?

Trees in churchyards may not be felled without the consent of the Diocesan Parsonages Board. An exception is when they become dangerous and involve some imminent risk; if such a case arises, the Archdeacon should be consulted (*see also* Chapter 4, *Churchyards and the Law*, p. 24).

Felling of large trees in confined spaces is a difficult and dangerous job which must be carried out by experts.

It is worth getting good advice before contemplating any felling, planting or lopping. Forestry Consultants exist and there are reputable tree surgeons and nurserymen. The Forestry Commission officers and foresters are ready to advise in an unofficial and friendly capacity. The Commission will at any rate suggest where to go for advice. In country districts many private or National Trust estates still employ woodmen or foresters who are very knowledgeable. Local authorities' parks departments will also be able to provide expert advice.

The planting of new trees and subsequent care of them is not difficult but requires forethought. The most important factor is probably scale. How will the tree look when it is fully grown? Will it be too close to the church or the churchyard boundary or adjoining houses? Will it harm existing memorials? Perhaps a small tree might be suitable where a big one would be out of place. If there is room, there is a lot to be said for planting big, long-lived trees, either individually or in groups or lines, which will provide beauty and pleasure for several centuries. In a small churchyard there are plenty of smaller but still beautiful species to choose from. With the considerable rise in the price of timber it may well be wise to invest by planting oak trees which will in sixty years provide the new church roof.

Whether evergreen or deciduous trees, conifers or broad-leaved should be chosen is a matter of judgement in individual circumstances. Trees should both harmonise and contrast with their surroundings and with each other. Deciduous trees have the advantage of looking different at each season of the year. Evergreens give shade, shelter and colour all the year round. If there is room for both, so much the better. Most broad-leaved trees are deciduous (exceptions being the holly and the holm oak or *ilex*) and autumn leaf fall may have to be dealt with by sweeping leaves off paths and out of gutters. But this is a small price to pay for the beauty of autumn colouring. Most conifers are evergreen (an exception is larch).

Individual tree species have different requirements as regards light and shade, soil, moisture or dryness, shelter or exposure and purity of air. There are many books available on the subject; some are listed at the end of this publication. It is not possible to deal here with individual species, but one or two notes may be useful.

The traditional churchyard tree is the yew, and many churchyards contain ancient yews which should be looked after. Some are important

87

historically. In mass they may strike some people as a little gloomy, but their dark green contrasts admirably with the building materials of our churches, and the tradition should be preserved. But it is worth remembering that on no account should livestock have access to yew trees (which should not therefore be allowed to overhang adjoining fields). Of other conifers, apart from the many decorative and garden varieties available, Scots pine is hardy and attractive when well grown. Cedars must have plenty of room and are slow growing, but old trees, especially cedars of Lebanon, can be magnificent and are worth considering. Cypresses are thought by many to be depressing but they have traditionally been associated with mourning for centuries and are not out of place in a churchyard.

As regards hardwoods, at one end of the scale are the big forest trees such as lime, beech, horse chestnut, maple and sycamore. Oak is the traditional English tree, but has no particular decorative virtues in this context. Elms (other than small weeping varieties) are unreliable in their habits and are best avoided. So are ash, which are not in leaf for many months and shed a great many twigs. Among the smaller trees, silver birch are almost always worthwhile, also whitebeam and rowan, and there are many decorative flowering cherries and almonds. The virtues of holly should not be overlooked, with dense shiny green leaves and (on female trees only) berries. Poplars are not much liked ('unpop'lar'!) near buildings—especially those built on shrinkable clay—because of a famous case, which every lawyer knows, where damages were awarded in respect of the effects of poplar roots on a next-door neighbour's house. But Black Poplars are lovely trees: there is one churchyard with hundred-year-old poplars now very large (too large) but so far, apparently, braving the gales without yielding. The commoner trees are not expensive to buy, at any rate not in small sizes, and it is worth noting that small trees are established much more easily than big. They may or may not require staking in their early years and protection from rabbits, hares, sheep and dogs. Protection *can* be expensive.

It is surprising and disturbing to discover how few people professing to be able to prune or pollard trees really understand how to do it. It might be useful for DACs and rural deans to compile lists of recommended firms or individuals.

The sylvicultural beauty of our churchyards over the next century depends upon the trouble we are prepared to take today. The planting and care of trees can be very rewarding.

88

20. Sheds and rubbish places

In its various published reports and pamphlets over the years the Council for Places of Worship has constantly stressed the need to keep the church building free from toolsheds, rubbish heaps and fuel-stores. All these things are necessary, but there is no need for the appearance of the church and churchyard to be spoiled by the erection of various temporary and makeshift structures, and ill-placed dumps, as is so often the case.

In many churches, fuel and tools are accommodated in a seemly and permanent manner under cover, either inside the boiler house, or in a screened-off portion of the vestry; but where they are not, what may be required is a small structure in a corner of the churchyard or against the churchyard wall, away from the church, to serve for tools or storage. There is no need for it to be expensive, though wood is no longer cheap, and it need not be made to look 'Gothic' or 'ecclesiastical'. Canadian red cedar makes a pleasant-looking shed if a good design is chosen, and the materials can readily be bought. This wood needs no preservative, and usually harmonizes well with its surroundings. Corrugated iron should be avoided.

It may be found impractical to provide a shed for solid fuel, which after all does not deteriorate with exposure, but in no case should fuel be allowed to stand against the church itself. Rainwater percolating through it is likely to produce a harmful chemical reaction which will soon destroy the stonework, and the heap itself will probably bridge any damp course.

The siting of storage tanks presents a problem to parishes converting to oil-fired heating. These tanks are necessarily large, but it is sometimes possible to find room for them in the former boiler house. If, however, a tank is to be sited actually in or under the church, it should be placed in a proper fire-resisting compartment and above a catchpit. If it is to be placed outside the church, in an existing lean-to compartment, care should be taken to ensure that there are no unprotected openings in the church wall at this point, which in case of a fire would permit the rapid spread of heat and fumes. If the tank is to be in the open air, it should be within a suitable catch-pit, preferably a few feet

89

away from the church to allow repainting. A position should be found which is inconspicuous, and not too far away from the boiler. It is not necessary for the tank to be placed in a prominent position near the road, since the tankers in which the fuel is delivered are equipped with long hoses. If, however, it is more than 80 or 90 feet (24 or 28 m) from the nearest point of access, it will probably be necessary to lay a filling-pipe to a point nearer the road.

The priming coat of paint which is usually applied when the tank is delivered is quite inadequate to prevent rust forming. It should be given two good coats of paint before it is fixed in position on blue brick or concrete piers. Bitumastic paint can be obtained in pleasant grey or dull russet shades and black. In most districts, however, it should be possible to select a suitable colour of oil paint from the Standard Colour Range BS 4800. Colour cards for the complete range are not easily available outside the building trade, but the inspecting architect should be able to provide suitable suggestions. Different stones or bricks will demand different approaches, and even within a single locality variations will occur in natural materials.

Water tanks should not be allowed to remain against the walls of churches, unless this is the only possible means of supply, as they frequently leak unnoticed and cause walls to become damp. Provision for water supply should preferably be made by a standpipe elsewhere in the churchyard. Sometimes, however, water can only be obtained by collecting it from the roof of a shed or of the church. The water is then often stored in a metal tank although suitably coloured plastic butts are now available, either without an overflow pipe, or with one which is inadequate. A good supply can be obtained if the tank is served by a 2½ inch (62 mm) or 3 inch (75 mm) rainwater pipe. An overflow pipe is essential and should never be less than 2 inches (50 mm) in diameter and should be brought down to a surface channel or rainwater gully. The tank should be set on brick supports in such a way that there is a slight fall away from the wall. An inconspicuous position should, of course, be chosen.

Rubbish is often allowed to accumulate far too long. It should be collected in a clearly identifiable spot, away from the church and well screened from view. Dead flowers and grass-clippings should be separately provided for, on a compost heap in a screened-off corner of the churchyard: the compost can then be used on any flower beds the churchyard may have. Other rubbish should be burned at frequent intervals and on a day when the wind is blowing away from the church. Bonfires should not be lit on, around, or near memorials. An incinerator may be required for the burning of wreaths. (Sometimes these are almost incombustible.) It is illegal to light an open fire within 50 feet (15 metres) of the public highway.

21. *Lighting and notice boards*

The approach to a church may be made or marred by its notice board or the churchyard lighting. These details are of such importance that they should be a matter for careful consideration in association with the church architect. The overall impact of church and churchyard needs always to be borne in mind.

Artificial lighting in the churchyard should be provided in a simple form. A plain lantern or a wall light on an oak post can be placed to light the pathway. Lights should not be fixed to the outside walls of churches or generally to a lych-gate; but if, because of wanton damage, a more substantial type of fitting is necessary bulkhead lights may be erected provided they are strongly fixed to the wall. Concrete lamp posts of most of the standard municipal types should be avoided. The best examples of currently available mass-produced lampstandards may be studied in the collection displayed at the Design Centre (Council for Industrial Design) Haymarket, London, S.W.1.

Old lamp frames over gates can be adapted to modern conditions but, for technical reasons of safety, this should be done only by a professional electrician. All new outdoor light fittings should be of non-ferrous metal to avoid rusting.

Great care needs to be taken about the flood-lighting of a church. No building was built to be illuminated from the ground—or from within—and it is often better to have lamps shining from the adjoining building. On the other hand, it is important that a flood-lighting scheme should take into account the relationship of the church with other buildings. Sometimes only certain features, such as the spire or tower, should be flood-lit. In every case the church architect should be consulted. It may be wise to illuminate a building only for certain occasions rather than to install a system permanently.

In the country it is often considered sufficient to exhibit notices in the church porch. The provision of adequate and accessible notice boards is especially important in united benefices or grouped parishes where the services may be at a variety of times. A notice giving 'Times of services' might also be exhibited elsewhere in the village—near the inn, the shop or the bus stop. Because of the increase in vandalism and thefts, many churches have to be kept locked, and at a time when more and more visitors are genuinely anxious to see inside them. It is *very* desirable, therefore, that a notice should indicate where the key may be obtained. This is especially important in case of fire.

It is probably sufficient simply to erect a free-standing notice board beside the gates of urban churches; and helpful if the notice board can be sited fairly near a lamp post so that it can be read at night. It is better to avoid siting notice boards under trees, and if this is unavoidable they need to be protected by a projecting top with a covering such as bituminous felt or lead. The posts should be painted with two coats of paint.

Black letters on a white or cream-coloured ground, or white on a background of dark blue, red, dark green or black show up best. If the board stands in the sun, blue tends to fade quickly. Gold letters or unpainted wood, or incised letters, are not easily read. There is no necessity to make the board look 'ecclesiastical' by means of Gothic lettering or crosses.

It is worth taking trouble over the information which the notice board is to convey. In many cases, particularly in the country, all that is needed is the name and dedication of the church, the times of regular services and the address and telephone number of the parish priest. Generally speaking, the briefer the wording the more effective the message. The design for a permanent notice board should be referred for advice to the DAC and be carried out by a professional or good amateur lettering artist.

The Town and Country Planning (Control of Advertisements) Regulations 1969 S.I. 1532 and 1974 S.I. 185 apply to church notice boards which are visible from the street or road so far as their structure and design are concerned. Notice boards in existence in 1948 are ordinarily exempt from control, and no express consent is required for one notice board (or two if the church has a frontage to more than one road or street) not exceeding 12 square feet or 1·2 square metres, nor for a temporary notice board, provided it is not erected more than 28 days before and is removed within 14 days after the event to which it relates. All notice boards are subject to standard conditions requiring them to be kept clean and tidy. It would be prudent to make enquiries from the local planning authority before incurring expense in providing a notice board not within the foregoing exemptions.

22. New churchyards

Before a parish decides to acquire a new churchyard or adds an extension to an old one, it is advisable to investigate thoroughly the possibility of re-using the existing area. Many parishes are already saddled with the upkeep of large extensions made in the nineteenth century. It is no longer the parish but the Local Authority which is responsible for the provision of a burial ground.

However, if it is decided to use or acquire further land for burial, planning permission must be obtained. The parish should take the opportunity of adopting rules to ensure its development as a place of unspoiled beauty. The incumbent's rights and duties in the supervision of memorials and their inscriptions apply as much in a new as they do in an existing churchyard.

The first consideration is the enclosing of the land, which should generally be by hedging or walling (wire fencing on concrete posts is not an acceptable alternative) and the provision of a simple, dignified entrance gate. The second consideration is good landscaping, and the layout of the graves will depend upon the nature of the overall design. If a formal layout is desired, this will require different treatment from a 'looser' layout in which, for instance, gravestones might follow the lines of the contours. The area should be planned with a minimum of paths. It is ideal if these follow a continuous circulatory system (a single circle is often sufficient) in order that the funeral party may proceed to any part of the new ground and return to the church again without difficulty. The spacing of the graves must ensure the most economical use of the ground consistent with good landscaping and render it easy to maintain.

By its very nature a new graveyard will have a considerable area unencumbered with gravestones for some time to come. A temporary fence might be erected within the main boundary, so that hay can be cropped or sheep grazed or the grass left long and spring bulbs planted. A totally unkempt area will spoil the appearance of the whole.

If the extension is away from the old churchyard, the provision of a free-standing and perhaps centrally placed cross will bear witness to its use as a place of Christian burial. The cross may be of stone or timber but whatever the material this is an opportunity of introducing something of permanent value and significance and it is worth taking a good deal of trouble to find the best solution. Thought should be given to the setting aside of an area for the interment of cremated remains. If a churchyard cross is erected in the new churchyard or extension then the area around the cross could be set aside for this and the base of the cross so designed that the names and dates of those whose cremated remains are interred could be inscribed there.

A few flowering trees, planted when the ground is being prepared, will help to soften the effect of new graves and monuments, but generally the trees should not be arranged symmetrically. Obviously it is difficult to generalise, and in many cases the advice of a landscape architect would be valuable. Seemly provision for rubbish should not be forgotten; a well-screened corner for discarded wreaths and flowers is essential.

Hitherto there have been many places where the opening of an addition to an existing churchyard required the approval of the Secretary of State for the Environment as a result of provisions in an Order in Council under the Burial Acts in force in the area. But the Secretary of State has been advised that provisions in existing Orders in Council imposing such a requirement have now ceased to be operative in view of the repeal of S.6 of the *Burial Act 1953* by the Local Government Act 1972 (*see* Circular 56/74 issued by the Department of the Environment, HMSO, price 9p). This does not, of course, affect the obligation to seek planning permission from the planning authority.

23. Disposal and commemoration of cremated remains

First of all it must be recalled what cremated remains are; though often referred to as 'ashes', they are not in fact ashes at all but purified, calcined bone. All that is subject to corruption has been effectively consumed by the 'cleansing power of the flame'.

It should be the normal practice for the cremated ashes of parishioners to be buried in the churchyard ground, in a part of the churchyard deliberately set aside for that purpose—yet not too rigidly defined by dwarf walls, beech hedges, a proliferation of rose bushes and the like. And burials should be in accordance with an orderly plan approved by the PCC from which departures, it should be made clear, are not permitted. A separate register should be kept of these interments. It must be noted that the *Local Authorities' Cemeteries Order 1974* requires that there should be no disturbance of cremated remains. The greatest care must therefore be taken over interring, as once buried they can only be removed under an exhumation order. Technically scattering of ashes therefore 'seals' the ground beneath.

As to the manner of disposal, it cannot be too strongly urged that caskets, of whatever kind, should be dispensed with at the moment of interment; in many churchyards (and, for instance, the cloister garths or other traditional places of interment associated with cathedrals) this is already a condition firmly laid down. A 'long-life' casket is of no benefit to anyone, except the supplier; and a 'short-life' casket (*e.g.* of cardboard) will only ensure that the remains tend to adhere together instead of being dispersed into the earth. Direct committal into the earth is, from the point of view both of symbolism and sound practical sense, the course to be preferred. The use of a polythene container is to be avoided as it is indestructible except by fire.

INTERMENT AREA

However, it is important to consider each aspect of this matter stage by stage, and the first step must be the setting apart of a specific area of the churchyard for the interment of cremated remains; in conjunction with this step it is necessary to decide upon a means whereby those interred in the area may be commemorated. A faculty will be needed—probably the same faculty can cover other aspects, such as the type of memorial and a display case for a *Book of Remembrance* in a church—and the advice of the DAC should be sought *before* finally deciding upon what terms to apply for a faculty. The director of the local crematorium may well be able to provide very useful advice. A delegation or representative of the DAC with particular knowledge or experience will also usually be willing to visit, and it is an advantage to have the stimulus of an informed outside point of view when deciding upon a matter which is likely to have a considerable effect on the total impact of the church and churchyard, and may involve the disturbance of existing graves or gravestones. All these matters, taken together, will affect the issues which concern a parish priest and church council in the care of their church and churchyard: pastoral, aesthetic and environmental. So it is important to find the best possible solution.

Having settled upon the area of the churchyard to be set apart, and having agreed upon the method of demarcation, which should be unobtrusive enough to enable this part of the churchyard to merge more or less imperceptibly into the remainder, the next step is to consider its surface treatment. Perhaps it is ideal if the grass of the area is kept reasonably smooth and short, but not necessarily to the extent that it will acquire the character of a garden lawn. Interments are then made, as in the grounds of many crematoria, under the turf.

While the setting aside of a special area for the interment of cremated remains invariably requires the authority of a faculty, the occasional isolated burial of cremated remains in a part of the churchyard normally used for the burial of bodies may in practice usually be done simply at the incumbent's discretion. Again, it is sometimes desired to bury remains in a grave already occupied by a body. This is likely to arise where, for instance, the children of a deceased couple wish to bury the cremated remains of one parent in the grave in which the other parent's body lies. There is no objection to this, if it is done at the relatives' request and the incumbent consents. But the ashes should be sprinkled in the hole excavated for the purpose (*see* below) and not buried in a casket.

MEMORIALS

The desire to commemorate and adorn the actual place of interment applies as much to ashes as to ordinary human remains. And whilst small posies, not in vases, may be permitted this does not satisfy the piety of many bereaved, who require the consolation of a visible memorial. Before any decision is taken the most careful thought must be given to the principles involved and the parochial church council should discuss all aspects of the problem with the DAC.

Possibly a most satisfactory type of memorial would be a scaled down version of a headstone, say not exceeding 2 feet 3 inches (675 mm) in height, but sufficient space is rarely available for this to become a practical proposition and if a section of the churchyard has been set aside for the commemoration of cremated remains, then some form of tablet or plaque is generally more appropriate. Where these are permitted they should be of natural quarried materials subject to the same regulations as other memorials regarding colour and finishes and we suggest should not exceed 1 foot 9 inches square (525 mm) nor be less than 1 foot (300 mm) square. The latter size is too small for good lettering but may have to be accepted if space is very limited, but 1 foot 6 inches by 1 foot (450 by 300 mm) is sufficient for a simple inscription, whilst the larger size would be required to include any originality and variety of design.

The simplest tablet is one set flush with or slightly below the level of the ground so that a mower could pass over it. Unfortunately water soon collects in such hollows and the inscription is obscured by mud when the water evaporates; grass soon creeps over the edges and settlement is rarely uniform. It is unfortunately no remedy to set the tablet at an angle for the rain will still collect at one end and if it is raised above the turf level the edges are liable to damage from the blades of a lawn mower. A possible solution may be not to have grass at all but to set the stones in gravel though this is quite an untraditional treatment of the surface of an English churchyard. Perhaps cover plants such as clover or saxifrage could be planted between stones. But though this course may alleviate the problems of encroaching verdure it does not solve the problem of rain water and uneven settlement; nor is there any provision for flowers.

One alternative is to set up a wedge-shaped tablet several inches above the ground, and say 1 foot 9 inches square mounted on a foundation set flush with the ground which will prevent lopsided settlement, allow the water to drain off, permit the mower to pass nearby with impunity; and if requested a vase might be incorporated in the design. However, there may be objections arising from the size of these stones in relation to other gravestones in the churchyard. Another alternative is to arrange interments along the side of a path whose kerbs are shaped to record the particulars of those whose ashes are buried adjacent. A third possibility is the building of a terrace of flagstones laid over concrete rails the centre lines of which should be the same distance apart as the length of the tablet so that all tablets can rest butt-jointed on the rails to prevent grass growing between. Interments are made under these flagstones which are then either incised or replaced by some other commemorative stone.

PRACTICALITIES

From what has been written above it will be clear that the introduction of tablets can create problems. It may even vitiate in part the purpose of cremation which is to reduce the area of land taken up by the dead; it may create even more maintenance problems. Whilst this suggestion would mark a completely new departure in churchyards, consideration might be given to the possibility that such memorials should be on a leasehold basis of say 25 years after which period they would be removed unless the lease were renewed. Note, that wherever re-use is contemplated care must be taken not to disturb the ashes already interred.

In a paper available from the Council for Places of Worship, *Churchyard monuments in the 20th century* (1973), Mr Laurence Whistler, well known as a writer, designer and engraver on glass, has suggested that where there is a churchyard wall, small inscriptions and sculpted panels might be placed on the inner face of the wall. This is not entirely a new suggestion, as something very like it exists in the loggia designed by the Victorian painter G. F. Watts in the churchyard of St Botolph, Aldersgate in the City of London, and a church in Yorkshire has experimented with a similar idea. Some may feel that such treatment of a wall might produce a 'postage stamp' effect, which could be monotonous and dull. Yet it might be attractive and interesting, provided always that variety were allowed, and good craftsmanship available. Anyone who has visited the Campo Santo at Pisa will know that a wall covered with inscriptions can be an object of interest and pleasure. Whether or not a faculty would be required for each individual panel would depend entirely upon the Diocesan Chancellor. But as, in spite of the precedents referred to earlier, the idea is a comparatively novel one it would be desirable to establish Diocesan Rules (as for headstones and other memorials in the churchyard) within which the incumbent would be free to exercise his own discretion. For instance to avoid too obvious a patchwork the material should preferably be stone or slate—*not* marble (whether black, white or coloured), nor any highly polished substance. A matt or semi-matt ceramic tablet of a suitable colour might be a welcome element of visual variety. A maximum size and thickness should be fixed. Then, these straightforward conditions accepted, there should be freedom of shape—square, oblong, round, diamond, and so forth—and freedom of style in decoration and lettering. As with headstones, good models will be valuable; a 'Pattern Book' for the design of memorials is to be produced by the Council for Places of Worship, including also some suggestions for mural tablets for churchyard walls. In the case of brick or ashlar-faced walls it may be appropriate to have the tablets inset, but in other cases the tablets will no doubt have to be affixed to the wall rather in the same way as internal monuments are fixed to the walls of the church.

We have indicated above a variety of methods for commemoration; and there is room for further experiment. However, in many parishes a *Book of Remembrance* will be the method chosen. Here it is advisable to consult with both the parish's architect and the DAC, for the book and the stand (probably with a glass top) on which it rests will contribute towards the total impact of the interior of the church itself. It seems unlikely that a stock product will provide the most sensitive and appropriate answer, and a stand made specially for the context in which it will be placed (and made, preferably, by a craftsman of some distinction) may be a real opportunity for enhancing and enriching the church at a point which will be of comfort to the bereaved and significance for the whole worshipping congregation. The best, incidentally, is not necessarily the most expensive. A well-designed recent example is illustrated in Figure 22. In the Book of Remembrance can be inscribed the names of all those whose ashes have been interred in the churchyard, the cost of the calligrapher's work being added to the fee charged for the interment. The names may be inscribed chronologically, or there may be a page for each day of the year with the book open each day at the appropriate page.

METHOD OF INTERMENT

Sufficient has already been said to make it plain that the use of caskets is not recommended. But what of the actual process of interment? It cannot be too strongly emphasised at this point that *burial* has always been the Christian tradition of decently interring the remains of the departed. 'Strewing' and 'scattering' can be unseemly and distressing to the bereaved and these methods should be eschewed. One suggestion is that (having devised an orderly plan for the placing of burial plots in the specially set aside area of the churchyard) a hole should be dug by means of a 6 inch (150 mm) earth auger or post-hole boring tool between 18 inches (450 mm) and 2 feet (600 mm) deep. The cremated remains will, of course, arrive in some kind of container from the crematorium and the remains should be gently poured into the hole and then *immediately* (to avoid any possible distress to the bereaved) a thin layer of earth sprinkled over the top. If there is a wish to have several interments in the same hole then a stout oak board should be placed over the layer of earth, and the remainder of the hole can be filled in on top of the board as soon as the service of committal has been concluded and the grave plot may then be turfed over. The point of the stout wooden board is that it avoids the possibility of either the cremated remains or the thin layer of soil being disturbed; and it also means that, when the next interment takes place, the topsoil can be removed down to the board, the board lifted up, and the whole process repeated. No ashes should be interred less than 4 inches (100 mm) below the surface of the soil. Clearly circumstances will vary from place to place, but this method is strongly recommended as being both seemly and economical in its use of space.

There can be no objection to the disposal of cremated remains in what is technically a closed churchyard (*i.e.* closed by Order in Council); occasions may only arise rarely, but if in doubt a faculty should be sought and is likely to be granted unless the churchyard is being cared for by the local authority and the local authority objects for any reason. Again, this seems unlikely.

It is not uncommon, particularly in urban situations, for a church to stand within an *unconsecrated curtilage*. If the church itself is consecrated then the presumption must be that the curtilage no less than the church is subject to the Faculty Jurisdiction. The bishop might be willing to consecrate the curtilage, if a sufficient need could be shown; but both the *Pastoral Measure 1968* and the secular legislation contain provisions enabling churchyards or curtilages, whether consecrated or not, to be devoted to secular purposes in certain circumstances so there is probably little point in doing this. In any case each situation must be judged entirely on its own merits, and in the first instance it would be wise to seek the advice of the Diocesan Registrar.

Disposal of cremated remains in consecrated buildings always, of course, requires a faculty and these are seldom granted. It is especially unlikely that a faculty would be granted, except in very special circumstances, for interment in a wall, and interments in the floor of a church should never be close to a wall or pillar. The church architect would need also to be consulted about heating or electrical ducts, any possible archaeological implications of disturbance of the floor, and so on. On the whole, therefore, this is firmly to be discouraged. The provision of a *Columbarium* in a crypt, if one exists, or in a separate building, is certainly a possibility; but if the columbarium is in the crypt it is likely to inhibit any other future use of that space, and to make it necessary to restrict access. And in a situation where the maintenance of church buildings is already a heavy burden on local Christian communities it scarcely needs pointing out that there is an inherent unwisdom in providing an additional building to maintain. Even if a substantial endowment were offered it is reasonable to assume that a conscientious parish priest might well direct the attention of the donor to an alternative and more urgently compassionate need. In short, the brief vogue for *Columbaria* now seems more or less entirely a thing of the past— though one or two fine ones exist, *e.g.* that designed by Sir Ninian Comper at St Peter's, Bournemouth—and few are likely to be established in normal parochial circumstances in the foreseeable future.

Since cremated remains are not the same as a body, slightly different legal considerations apply, and these are dealt with in Chapter 4, *Churchyards and the law*, to which readers are referred.

Schemes for setting aside a portion of the churchyard for the disposal of ashes should always be thought out in careful detail—perhaps by setting up a special sub-committee of the PCC to consider the matter, and certainly in close consultation with the DAC—and then be submitted with a petition for a faculty.

The crematorium will, as a matter of course, fulfil the requirements of the law which relate to the cremation. So far as the parish church is concerned the burial register should on no account be used, since ashes are not the same as a body; but orderliness and good management demand that every parish church should keep a register for recording the interment of ashes whenever this occurs and the only practicable solution is to establish a special one for this purpose.

24. Registers, records and insurance

There are five principal documents which relate to the churchyard. They are:

1. The burial register.
2. The register of the disposal of cremated remains.
3. The log book to be kept under the *Inspection of Churches Measure 1955*.
4. The register of stones and inscriptions.
5. The Terrier and Inventory. (An official format is published by the Church Information Office.)

The burial register A standard format is laid down, which is the same in every parish. It is a good practice, however, to put in the margin the reference letter and number of the grave, which should agree with the letter and number on the plan of the churchyard.

The register of the disposal of cremated remains The official registration of the disposal of the body has been made at the crematorium, but it is proper that the parish should have some record of parishioners whose ashes have been buried. The record should have (a) the full name of the deceased; (b) the former home address; (c) the date of burial (d) the reference to the grave if buried in the churchyard, or the place of disposal, if not; (e) the name of the officiating minister.

The log book has to be kept under the *Inspection of Churches Measure 1955* and should include, in addition to details of repairs to the church and its contents, any work on the gates, hedges, walls, paling or paths of the churchyard, with brief details of work carried out, name and address of contractor and architect, and so on.

The register of stones and inscriptions has been largely dealt with in an earlier section (see Chapter 12 on *Recording the churchyard*). This register and its accompanying plan should be kept with other registers, and from it copies of inscriptions may be supplied to relatives on request. An index is of great value.

The Terrier and Inventory may record gravestones of particular interest. The importance of preserving all registers, plans and other documents cannot be too strongly emphasised. They are now recognised as public and national records of the highest value. Good ink should always be used—never a 'ball' or similar pen. If the safe containing the registers shows signs of dampness, a tin of special absorbent material called silica gel, may be purchased for a small sum from Silica Gel Ltd, 62 Shaftesbury Avenue, London, W.1., and if kept in the safe will take up the moisture. It is wise to open the safe frequently and to swing the door a few times to circulate air, and the books should be taken out occasionally for dusting and airing.

Many registers date from the sixteenth century and are in almost perfect preservation. Few, indeed, are the churchyard monuments which have come down from that time. When consideration is given to the demand which is made from monuments of the most enduring materials on the one hand and on the other the difficulty of securing the permanence of an inscription in stone, it can well be seen how valuable is a system of recording such as we have outlined.

There is also the possibility of using a *Record Card* and a specimen is given in Appendix VI(a) which has been evolved and found eminently useful in the parish of Penn, Bucks.

Books of Remembrance provide a very useful alternative to outdoor and indoor memorials in stone. The book should be strongly bound and housed in the church on a well-designed lectern or in a ventilated glass case. Whilst carved inscriptions must be short, it is possible to allow perhaps half a page for a full entry in the book, provided that appropriate payment is made for the calligraphy. All entries should be made by the same professional calligrapher in order to preserve uniformity of style. To the cost of writing should be added a small sum for the insurance and renewal of the book itself. The Diocesan Advisory Committee should be consulted on the design and position of the lectern, for which a faculty is required.

INSURANCE

It is advisable for every parochial church council to take out a third-party or public liability insurance policy; the premium is small and it covers the parochial church council against claims arising from accidents to persons using the church and churchyard, whether lawfully or as trespassers. The Civil Courts are now awarding very heavy damages against parties proved guilty of any neglect in such cases. The policy should cover the incumbent as well as the parochial church council.

Apart from insuring against legal liability many parochial church councils have taken out Group Insurance Policies which would provide a modest sum in the event of a church volunteer suffering serious injury or loss of earnings. Details can be obtained from the Ecclesiastical Insurance Office Ltd.

(From *It Won't Happen to Us*, a pamphlet on church insurance published for The Council for Places of Worship by C I O.)

25. Assistance from local authorities

GENERAL POWER TO CONTRIBUTE TOWARDS EXPENSES

The *Local Government Act 1972* Section 214(6) provides as follows:
> A burial authority may contribute towards any expenses incurred by any other person in providing or maintaining a cemetery in which the inhabitants of the authority's area may be buried.

'Burial Authorities' are defined in Section 214(1) to include not only district councils and parish councils but also the councils of London boroughs and of communities as well as parish meetings of parishes having no parish council and the Common Council of the City of London. 'Cemetery' includes a burial ground or any other place for the interment of the dead (including any part of any such place set aside for the interment of a dead person's ashes).

This is a wide power replacing the former provision in the *Parish Councils Act 1957* but its exercise is not, of course, confined to closed churchyards.

CLOSED CHURCHYARDS

In the case of churchyards closed for burials (whether with or without exceptions permitting certain burials to take place) by Order in Council, Section 215 of the Local Government Act 1972 provides that the parochial church council shall maintain the churchyard by keeping it in decent order and its walls and fences in good repair. But the parochial church council may transfer the obligation to the appropriate local authority by serving a written request to that effect. The request will normally be served upon the parish or community council or the district or London borough council in whose area the churchyard is situated, and the obligation to maintain the churchyard will be transferred to the appropriate local authority three months after the serving of the request. The former provision about repayment of expenses incurred by a parochial church council has ceased to apply save in the City of London (*see* generally Appendix IX, *Closed churchyards*). Closed churchyards remain subject to the Faculty Jurisdiction.

Where responsibility for the maintenance of a closed churchyard had been transferred to a local authority before April 1974 under the old law, the *Local Authorities (Miscellaneous Provisions) Order 1974* (S.I.482) Article 16, provides that the future responsibility for its maintenance shall rest upon the local authority upon whom a request under Section 215 would fall to be served, which in most cases will be the parish council or the district council which has succeeded to the obligations of the former authority.

CARE AND MANAGEMENT OF A BURIAL GROUND AS SUCH

Section 9(b) of the *Open Spaces Act 1906* (which should not be confused with provision in that Act for the use of disused burial grounds as open spaces) gives local authorities power to agree to undertake the entire or partial care and management of a burial ground as such (*i.e.* without laying it out as an open space and while permitting burials to continue). Though probably not appropriate for a churchyard surrounding a church in use, this provision might be beneficially used in the interests of amenity or to prevent a scandal in the case of a detached churchyard or one of the church burial grounds established in the nineteenth century the use of which was confined to members of the Church of England (*see* Halsbury's *Laws of England*, Fourth Edition 1975. Volume 10, title 'Cremation and Burial', p. 507), where some burials still take place and no funds or only inadequate funds are available for maintenance. Such assets as are available for general maintenance in such a case could be transferred to the local authority under Section 1(2) of the *Parish Councils and Burial Authorities (Miscellaneous Provisions) Act 1970*.

ANCIENT MONUMENTS

Local authorities have power to contribute towards preserving and maintaining structures in churchyards recognised as ancient monuments under the *Ancient Monuments Acts 1913 to 1953*, *e.g.* memorials, mausolea, sundials, lych-gates etc, whether they have become guardians of the monument or not, subject to the work to be undertaken being approved by the Department of the Environment.

WAR MEMORIALS

Local authorities have power to incur reasonable expenditure on the maintenance, repair and protection of war memorials, whether vested in them or not, under the *War Memorials (Local Authorities Powers) Act 1923* as amended.

Appendix I

A SUGGESTED PROCEDURE FOR CARE OF THE CHURCHYARD

(1) The parochial church council should adopt by formal resolution a set of rules covering the use and maintenance of the churchyard, following the lines of those given in Appendix II and with particular reference to any rules or regulations which may have been laid down by the chancellor of the diocese.

(2) A framed copy of these rules should be displayed in the church porch, together with an indication that:

(a) advice about suitable stones, appropriate design and the composition of inscriptions may be obtained from the incumbent (or some other person).

(b) *Before* permission is given to a stonemason, the design, with the inscription properly set out in the style of lettering to be used and with full particulars of the material, dimensions and proposed foundation work for setting up the stone, must be submitted to the incumbent for his approval, which must be obtained *in writing*.

(3) The rules, and a copy of the resolution of the parochial church council covering their adoption, should be sent to local monumental masons; they should also be individually informed of the necessity of obtaining the incumbent's approval *in writing*.

(4) An account should be established for the maintenance of the churchyard and the money deposited. Bequests of £50 or £100 or more should be invited, through the parish magazine or the local press, from all who expect to be buried in the churchyard. A collecting plate labelled 'Churchyard Maintenance Fund' might be placed near the church door at funerals, and a special house-to-house collection made at All Saints-tide. (For a house-to-house collection permission is required from the district council.)

(5) A member of the PCC with a small committee might be appointed to administer this fund and relieve the incumbent of responsibility. If the local authority contributes towards the maintenance of the churchyard (*see* Chapter 25), one or two of its members might be co-opted to this committee. In addition to the PCC and the local authority it is important to establish a working partnership with the actual facilities directly concerned, and to harness the voluntary help of a cross-section of the parish.

(6) A successful scheme has been in operation over a considerable period at Penn, in Buckinghamshire, and the special committee established here is called the *Churchyard Guild*—much of the detailed administrative work and correspondence with the next of kin being delegated to its secretary.

(7) If a fund is established for churchyard maintenance the PCC should establish a Trust Deed in association with the Diocesan Board of Finance, so that capital monies for long-term upkeep can be lodged for investment (v. Appendix V (a)). The Investment Fund of the Central Board of Finance of the Church of England is a suitable medium, and the interest can now be paid quarterly. In addition the PCC should open a special churchyard fund account, and arrange with the bank that the outstanding balance at the end of each month shall be transferred automatically into their general account. This avoids the need for a separate treasurer, as all outgoings are thereby

made through the PCC treasurer, following the advice and directions of the incumbent and guild secretary.

(8) A scale of standard annual contributions towards the upkeep of the churchyard generally should be fixed by the PCC e.g. £5 p.a. (which would be approximately 5p per week for grave maintenance and 5p for general churchyard upkeep and capital costs). The use of banker's order forms and deeds of covenant should be encouraged.

(9) The incumbent should invite the churchyard guild or committee to share in the work generally, and its members should cover a wide cross-section of the parish as a whole. They can help provide continuity of policy over a period of years. From time to time working parties of men, women and children too, should be encouraged —the object being to involve as many individuals as possible.

(10) A plan of the churchyard drawn to scale and showing the whereabouts of individual graves is an essential requirement. Each grave should be given a number in its plot or section (see Chapter 12, Recording the churchyard).

(11) A comprehensive card index recording all burials and memorials is also equally desirable both for present usage and for future reference. Each card should ideally show date of death, age, date of funeral, burial register number, names and addresses of next of kin and their relationship, type of memorial, plot and grave numbers; also names and addresses of the family solicitors, bankers and executors to enable contact to be maintained over the long term. Obviously such records would include a note as to whether a family made their contributions through an annual subscription, banker's order, deed of covenant or lump sum.

Appendix II

Before adopting these Rules parochial church councils should study Chapters 1, 5, 10 and 12 with care, and consult the registrar of the diocese as to whether they conform with the directions of the chancellor of the diocese.

GENERAL

1. The surface of the churchyard should be kept level as far as possible and free from grave mounds so that the grass may be cut by a mower.

2. Every application to erect or place anything whatsoever or do any works in the churchyard shall be made in writing in the first place to the incumbent, stating a full description of the proposed work including (as may be appropriate) designs, measurements, inscriptions and the like particulars. In any case where the authority of a faculty is required, the application shall be made to the registrar of the diocese.

3. Nothing shall be erected or placed in the churchyard until such proposals have received the consent of the incumbent in writing, or until a faculty has been received, as the case may be.

MONUMENTS

4. The incumbent will normally be able to sanction the erection of the following classes of monuments without the authority of a faculty:

(a) Headstones no larger than 4 ft (1200 mm) high, 3 ft (900 mm) wide and 6 in (150 mm) thick nor less than 2 ft 6 in (750 mm) high, 1 ft 8 in (500 mm) wide and 3 in (75 mm) thick.

NOTE: A base forming an integral part of the design of a headstone is permitted provided it does not project more than 2 in (50 mm) beyond the headstone in any direction and provided that it is fixed on a foundation slab (which may be of any suitable material, not necessarily natural quarried material) which itself is fixed flush with the ground and extending 3 to 5 in (75 to 125 mm) all round so that a mower may freely pass over it.

(b) Horizontal ledgers either flush with the turf or raised not more than 9 in (225 mm) above a base, extending not less than 3 in (75 mm) all round and itself flush with the turf. Inclusive measurements not more than 7 ft (2100 mm) by 3 ft (900 mm).

(c) Vases not more than 12 by 8 by 8 in (300 by 200 by 200 mm) with a memorial inscription.

(d) Where an area of the churchyard has already been set aside by faculty for the purpose, tablets or plaques for cremated remains not exceeding 1 ft 9 in (450 mm) square.

5. All such monuments should be made of teak or oak or of natural stone with no mirror polished surfaces (*i.e.* highly polished so as to reflect). Stones traditionally used in local buildings, or stones closely similar to them in colour and texture, are to be preferred.

6. A cross should be individually designed, if a permanent memorial in this form is desired. It is not, however, appropriate that there should be undue repetition of the supreme Christian symbol and the authority of a faculty is required.

THE SWARD

7. Bulbs and small annual plants may be planted in the soil of any grave.

8. Plants or flowers may be placed in a removable sunken container, preferably of unpolished aluminium.

9. Wreaths and cut flowers may be laid direct on any grave or set in vases or containers as above. Persons deputed to care for the day-to-day upkeep and maintenance of the churchyard may remove the same when they appear to be withered. No artificial flowers whatsoever shall be allowed.

SPECIFIC EXCEPTIONS

10. No black, or all-polished 'granite' of whatever colour, no white marble, synthetic stone or plastic.

11. No raised kerbs, railings, plain or coloured stone chippings, built-in vase containers, figure statuary, open books, bird baths.

12. No advertisement or trademark shall be inscribed on a gravestone. The mason's name may be inscribed at the side or the reverse of the headstone in unpainted and unleaded letters no larger than ½ in (15 mm), in height.

Appendix III

APPLICATION FORM FOR THE ERECTION OF A TOMBSTONE

BARCHESTER DIOCESE

APPLICATION

BY   DATE

FOR PERMISSION TO

CHURCHYARD   GRAVE NO.
GRAVE OF

DETAILS OF PROPOSED MEMORIAL
See over for dimensioned sketch

MATERIAL   COLOUR

FINISH

OVERALL SIZES (height first)

VASE (description & sizes)

PROPOSED INSCRIPTION(S)

APPROVED   DATE   FEES £ .

For Applicant's Use

Appendix IV

HOW TO DESTROY IVY, VALERIAN, BRAMBLE AND OTHER HARMFUL PLANTS

A growth of ivy or valerian, of brambles or of sapling roots which has become lodged against walls or monuments, can do a deal of damage. For killing them, it is suggested that 2,4,5-trichlorphenoxyacetic acid (2,4,5-T) in the form of its ester should be used in vaporising or diesel oil. This chemical is obtainable in proprietary preparations known usually as 'brushwood killers'. The plants should first be cut low to economise the use of fairly expensive material. This should be done after the season's growth has well started. The solution should be applied to the plants themselves and the soil, saturated over a diameter of about 3 feet (900 mm) to administer a lethal dose to the roots and any incipient suckers. This should prevent the throwing up of further suckers but, should this happen, a spot application of the solution the following year should suffice to complete the eradication.

Care should be taken to avoid splashing stonework, since the oil used as a vehicle will cause a nasty stain for some years. No physical harm will be done to the stonework, but it may look unsightly for a time. Care should also be taken to avoid wind-drift or the vaporising of the active ingredient. A still evening is the best time for application, to avoid the risk of hurting other plants and trees which may be in the vicinity.

Sodium chlorate may also be used effectively in these cases as a strong solution. This is a complete herbicide and will kill anything in the treated area. It should therefore not be used under trees, for the roots of a tree spread out as far as its branches. But in areas free from tree roots this complete destruction is often the only practical way of dealing with clumps of bramble. The treatment will occasion an unsightly bare patch for about four months. After this, the area may be seeded with lawn grass. If there is fine grass of the fescue type in the vicinity, this will usually gain first hold by natural seeding, since it is quick seeding and surface rooting. It is therefore often wise to leave nature to re-seed after sodium chlorate treatment in spring or early summer. Sodium chlorate itself presents a fire risk and in contact with organic materials may be explosive in moderate bulk. It is therefore wise to purchase a proprietary formulation which will usually incorporate a fire-resistant material. Care should be taken to avoid contaminating stone walls or stone memorials with the sodium chlorate solution.

Plants, especially ivy, should not be pulled off walls as their strong grip may pull out mortar and damage the masonry. They are better left to wither after cutting and poisoning the roots.

Other plants may be treated with selective herbicides, as noted under *Maintaining the churchyard* (page 54).

Algae, mosses and lichens can be destroyed by application of a copper solution. In its simplest form this consists of 1 oz of copper sulphate (obtainable from any chemist) dissolved in a gallon of water. (This is approximately 30 gms to 5 litres.) A better alternative is to make a stock solution of 16 gm copper carbonate in 180 ml (1 oz in a little over half a pint) of strong (0.88 sp gr) ammonia, adding water to make 2·5 litres (about half a gallon), and then to dilute this to make 22·5 litres (5 galls) of solution when required. It would be wise to have the stock solution made up by a chemist, since strong ammonia is capable of giving a nasty burn before dilution. Care should be taken to keep either solution away from metalwork. On stonework a test should be made, since there may be slight, but undesirable, staining of light-coloured stones.

Appendix V (a)

MODEL TRUST DEED FOR THE UPKEEP OF GRAVES

THIS DEED is made the Seventeenth day of February One thousand nine hundred and BETWEEN THE PAROCHIAL CHURCH COUNCIL OF in the Diocese of (hereinafter called 'the Council') of the one part and THE DIOCESAN BOARD OF FINANCE incorporated under the Companies Acts not for profit whose registered office is situate at Diocesan Church House (hereinafter called 'the Board') of the other part

WHEREAS the Council has recently paid to the Board the sum of pounds to be invested and held by the Board upon the trusts and with and subject to the powers and provisions hereinafter specified and declared of and concerning the same which said sum of pounds TOGETHER WITH all gifts legacies bequests and donations whether money or other property received by the Council or the Board as an addition thereto and the investments from time to time representing the same are hereinafter referred to as 'the Trust Fund'

AND WHEREAS it has been agreed that the management of the trust shall be vested in the Council as Administrative Trustees so long as the Council are entitled to the income thereof

NOW THIS DEED WITNESSETH AND IT IS HEREBY AGREED AND DECLARED as follows:

1. THE Board shall stand possessed of the Trust Fund upon the trusts and for the charitable ecclesiastical purposes hereinafter provided

2. THE Board shall pay the income of the Trust Fund to the Council to be applied by the Council for the purposes and in the manner hereinafter provided so long as the Council is entitled to receive the same

3. THE income of the Trust Fund shall be applied by the Council for the general upkeep of the Churchyard of the Church of in the said Parish

4. PROVIDED ALWAYS that in so far as any part of the Trust Fund has been or shall be contributed subject to a condition that a particular grave situate in the said Churchyard is kept in clean and proper order and condition then if for a period of twelve consecutive months such grave is not so kept the capital sum whether money or securities representing such part of the Trust Fund shall be held for the Board

115

absolutely to be applied in or towards carrying on the charitable objects of the Board or any of them

5. A Certificate signed when required by the Rural Dean that any grave is maintained in clean and proper order and condition shall be sufficient evidence in that behalf and any question as to the breach of the requirements that any grave shall be so kept shall be finally settled by him

6. THE receipt of the Treasurer of the Council for any income paid over to the Council by the Board shall be a sufficient discharge to the Board for the same

7. THE Board may at any time instead of paying the said income to the Council permit the Council to receive the same or may pay or cause the same to be paid into the banking account of the Council to be applied in the same manner as if it had been paid to the Council and any such receipt by permission or by payment into the said banking account shall discharge the Board from the same and the Board shall under no circumstances be liable or responsible to see to the application of any moneys paid to or received by the Council or paid into such account as aforesaid or for the acts or defaults of any bank with which any such banking account as aforesaid shall be kept

8. THE Board may invest the Trust Fund or any part thereof in or upon such shares stocks funds securities or other investments in any part of the world as the Board shall in its absolute discretion think fit and so that the Board shall be empowered to invest vary and transpose the investment of trust moneys in the same unrestricted manner as if it were the beneficiary or entitled to all such moneys

IN WITNESS whereof the Chairman and two other members of the Council on behalf of the Council have hereunto set their respective hands and seals and the Board has caused its Corporate Seal to be hereunto affixed the day and year first before written

SIGNED SEALED AND DELIVERED by
              being the Chairman and
                                and
being two other members of the Council
on behalf of the Council in
the presence of:

THE CORPORATE SEAL OF THE
DIOCESAN BOARD OF FINANCE was
hereunto affixed in the presence
of:

                                        Members

              Secretary

Appendix V (b)

THE   Diocesan Board of Finance hereby acknowledges the receipt from   of the sum of £   ** to be held upon trust to pay the income to the (Parochial Church Council) (Incumbent) of the Parish of   in the County of   and the Diocese of   for the maintenance of the church and churchyard of the said Parish so long as the grave of   in such churchyard is kept in good order and repair. From and after any breach of this condition coming to their knowledge the said Board shall hold the said sum and the investments representing the same and the income thereof for the general purposes of the Board. A Certificate signed every three years by the Rural Dean that the said grave is so kept shall be sufficient evidence in that behalf and any question as to breach of this condition shall be finally settled by him.

Note. Gifts in either of these forms create valid charitable trusts subject to a condition (upkeep of a specified grave) which is not charitable, and to pass a gift over in the event of a breach of that condition. Money spent on maintenance of a grave is not applied for charitable purposes. It is important therefore that the whole of the trust income be applied for the maintenance of the churchyard as a whole and that the specified grave be maintained in repair from other sources in the hands of the recipient of the trust income.

** The sum of money should provide an income amply sufficient to keep the grave in order, so as to enable the condition of the trust to be fulfilled without difficulty.

Appendix V (c)

MODEL FORM OF RECEIPT FOR A GIFT
inter vivos
FOR UPKEEP OF GRAVES IN PERPETUITY
(for use by PCCs)

THE PAROCHIAL CHURCH COUNCIL of the Parish of
in the Diocese of   HEREBY ACKNOWLEDGES the receipt
of   from
to be applied by the said Council upon the Trusts of a Deed of Declaration of
Trust for the upkeep of the Churchyard of the Church of
dated the   day of   and made between the said Council
of the one part and The   Diocesan Board of Finance of the
other part and the said Council FURTHER ACKNOWLEDGES that the Proviso
in Clause 4 of the said Declaration of Trust shall apply in relation to the grave of
in the said Churchyard.

DATED THE   day of

Treasurer of the Parochial
Church Council

Appendix V(d)

MODEL FORM OF LEGACY FOR UPKEEP OF GRAVES

I GIVE THE SUM OF £   free of duty to the
Diocesan Board of Finance Upon Trust to pay the income to the (Parochial Church
Council) (Incumbent) of the Parish of   in the County of
          and Diocese of   for the maintenance of the
church and churchyard of the said Parish so long as the grave of
in such churchyard is kept in good order and repair. From and after any breach of this
condition coming to the knowledge of the said Board I direct that the said Board shall
hold the said sum and the investments representing the same and the income thereof
for the general purposes of the Board. A Certificate signed every three years by the
Rural Dean that the said grave is so kept shall be sufficient evidence in that behalf and
any question as to breach of this condition shall be finally settled by him.

Appendix VI(a)

MODEL INDEX-CARD FOR RECORDING BURIALS IN A CHURCHYARD
(As used at Penn, Bucks)

Date of Death   Age   Date of Burial   Burial Reg. No.

(1)

(2)

Names and Addresses   Relationship

Next of Kin:

Family:

Memorial   Plot   Grave No.

Guild: Ann. Sub.   Cov.   Upkeep in Perpetuity

Solicitor

Bankers

Executor

Appendix VI(b)

MODEL GRAVE OR MEMORIAL RECORDING FORM

CEMETERY or GRAVEYARD

DEDICATION

1   NAT. GRID REF.

2   DATE of RECORD

3   NAME of RECORDER or GROUP

4   MEMORIAL No and LETTER

5   No. of COMPONENTS

6   ASSOCIATED FORM LETTERS

7   Memorial type: 1. flat   2. head   3. tomb   4. foot   5. other

8   GEOLOGY

9   STONE MASON or UNDERTAKER

10   Which faces are inscribed?—compass points

11   No. of people commemorated

12   TECHNIQUE of INSCRIPTION

13   Condition of monument: 1. sound, *in situ*   2. sound displaced
     3. leaning or falling apart   4. collapsed   5. overgrown

14   Condition of inscription: 1. mint   2. clear but worn
     3. mainly decipherable   4. traces   5. illegible or destroyed

15   DIMENSIONS   Height

16   (in mms)   Width

17   Thickness

18   PHOTOGRAPH NEGATIVE No.

19   ORIENTATION   1 (N)

which way stone faces

Front of Form

PHOTOGRAPH INSCRIPTION

REMARKS

Back of Form

122

Appendix VII

RIGHTS OF WAY OVER CHURCHYARDS—WAYLEAVES

No right of way, public or private, can exist in law over consecrated ground unless the dedication or grant is authorised by a faculty, but in an appropriate case, when the right has existed for a long time, the grant of a faculty that has been lost may be presumed. Some footpaths through churchyards have been recorded by local authorities as rights of way under the National Parks and Access to the Countryside Act 1949 as amended by the Countryside Act 1968 and the Local Government Act 1972, Section 184 and Schedule 17. Incumbents and parochial church councils should examine the draft or definitive maps prepared under the Act by their local authorities, and take all possible steps to ensure that no footpaths over their churchyards are erroneously recorded as rights of way. This should be treated as a matter of importance, as it may prevent much confusion in the future.

Where the public are permitted to use footpaths through a churchyard as a matter of grace, it is important to take adequate steps to prevent a presumption of dedication arising. This can be done by closing the footpath one day a year or by exhibiting a notice in the churchyard or depositing a plan with the local authority under Section 34 of the Highways Act 1959. If the method of depositing a plan is used, care must be taken to follow it up by a statutory declaration every six years.

Similarly, if the Post Office or the Area Electricity Board desire to erect poles in the churchyard, application should be made for a faculty to do so. The erection of poles can easily spoil the amenities of the churchyard and it may well be that, if the matter is dealt with in this way, some alternative position for them will be found. The local authority may in any case require this if the churchyard forms part of a conservation area. The laying of cables or drains, of course, requires a faculty.

Appendix VIII

LITTER IN CHURCHYARDS

Litter, small and large, tends to get thrown into churchyards because of proximity to the highways. The law as contained in the Litter Acts of 1958 and 1971 makes it a punishable offence for anyone to deposit litter without proper authority 'into or from any place in the open air to which the public are entitled to have access without payment'. A churchyard is such a public place even if the gates are temporarily locked.

Further protection is given by the Civic Amenities Act of 1967 which forbids the deposit of larger objects such as cars, refrigerators, cookers, and washing machines. A local authority under Section 20 is required to remove and dispose of such litter, which is regrettably to be found in churchyards in some industrial areas. It should be noted that both the Litter Act and the Civic Amenities Act require information to be laid within six months of an alleged offence.

Confetti is a problem in many churchyards, particularly where there are gravel paths and the paper is trodden in. The 'proper authority' in charge of a churchyard is the incumbent and churchwardens, who may permit or forbid it as they please. Outside the churchyard gates the responsibility and choice is that of the Local Authority. In 1960 the Sedburgh local Health Committee's recommendation that confetti be banned was rejected by the rural district council. Other authorities hold that where this practice has been traditional for many years, and not specifically forbidden, there should be no restrictions.

Appendix IX

CLOSED CHURCHYARDS

(Extracts reprinted by kind permission of the Legal Advisory Commission from the Fifth Edition of the *Opinions of the Legal Board* as amended.)

Closed Churchyards

1. Meaning of 'closed churchyard'. A 'closed churchyard' is generally taken to mean a churchyard which has been closed for burials by an Order in Council under Burial Acts, and the term is used in that sense in this opinion. A churchyard may have been entirely disused for many years but it would not on that account be described as a closed churchyard, nor would a churchyard where all further burials have been prohibited by a local Act of Parliament be so described.

On the other hand the fact that a churchyard is a closed churchyard does not necessarily mean that no burials may legally take place there as this will depend upon the exact terms of the Order (or Orders) in Council applicable to it. In some, all further burials are entirely prohibited; in others, the burial of relatives of those already buried in the churchyard may take place, subject to there being three, four or five feet (900, 1200, 1500 mm) of soil between the coffin lid and the surface of the ground: occasionally, with a tender regard for the individual, the Order provides that the burial of a named person shall be permitted. Burials in vaults are often excepted subject to special conditions. Sometimes part of a churchyard is closed.

2. Tracing Orders in Council. If a parochial church council or a local authority are not sure whether a particular churchyard has been closed or not, or wish to find the exact terms of the Order in Council, the following lines of enquiry are suggested:

(a) There will probably be a copy of the Order in Council or of the issue of the London Gazette in which it appeared, in the church chest, or with the local authority's records;

(b) The Index to the London Gazette 1839-1883 (available in the bigger reference libraries) will mention the Order if made before 1884;

(c) If made between 1884 and 1891 it could be traced through the quarterly indices to the London Gazette;

(d) If made after 1891, the Order will be listed at the end of the annual volumes of Statutory Rules and Orders or Statutory Instruments but this involves a tiresome search unless the approximate year is known;

(e) Enquiries may be made from the Department of the Environment, 2 Marsham Street, London SW1.

3. New Orders in Council. Most of the Orders in Council for the discontinuance of burials (with or without exceptions or qualifications) in churchyards were made in the middle of the nineteenth century for the protection of the public health at a time when open sewers and the absence of a piped water supply made it particularly important to prevent the seepage of offensive matter from decomposing bodies into

wells or streams likely to be used for drinking water. But Section 1 of the Burial Act 1853 does not in fact restrict the making of closing Orders to cases where this is necessary for the protection of the public health. The legal advisers of the Ministry of Housing and Local Government (as it then was) have agreed with the Legal Board's view of the law, but in practice the Secretary of State for the Environment almost invariably has only made representations to Her Majesty in Council for the making of a closing order where he is satisfied that discontinuance of burials, with or without exceptions or qualifications, is necessary for reasons of public health, thus adhering to the practice of his predecessors, namely, the Minister of Health, the Local Government Board and the Home Secretary.

This does not mean that no closing orders are made today, and between 1949 and 1974, about 189 Orders in Council have been made for the discontinuance of burials in churchyards, but Orders never have been made for the sole purpose of relieving the ecclesiastical authorities of the burden of maintaining a churchyard.

Notice of the representation which the Minister proposes to make and of the date when it will be considered by the Privy Council must be given in the London Gazette and by notices affixed to the doors of the churches affected, and notice is also given to the incumbent and to the local authority. This does not mean that the Ministry seek the consent of the local authority; the notice is sent to them because they have succeeded to the civil powers of the vestry to whose clerk notice had to be sent under Section 1 of the Burial Act 1853.

4. *Former restriction on the making of closing orders.* The former prohibition on making an Order in Council closing a burial ground which had been opened with the approval of the Secretary of State has been abolished by the Local Government Act 1972, Schedule 26, paragraph 15.

5. *Procedure for transferring responsibility for maintenance.* From 1 April 1974 Section 215 of the Local Government Act 1972 has now provided a much simpler procedure for a parochial church council to request a local authority to take over the maintenance of a closed churchyard, and Section 18 of the Burial Act 1855 (except in its application to the City of London) and Section 269 of the Local Government Act 1933 have been repealed from that date and past expenditure on a churchyard can no longer be reclaimed.

6. *What is involved in the maintenance and repair of closed churchyards by a local authority?* When the responsibility for a closed churchyard is transferred to a local authority they succeed to the functions and liabilities of the parochial church council. Section 215 of the Local Government Act 1972 lays down that the parochial church council shall maintain the churchyard by keeping it in decent order and its walls and fences in good repair. It is generally relatively easy to determine what is involved in the necessary repair of walls and other fences, but it is sometimes hard to determine what is involved in maintaining the churchyard 'in decent order'. According to Prideaux's *Churchwardens Guide*, 16th Edition, the duty of churchwardens (which would seem to apply to a church council and a local authority) is:

'. . . to see that the churchyard is kept in a decent and fitting manner, that it be cleared of all rubbish, muck, thorns, shrubs and anything else that may annoy parishioners when they come into it. . . .'

It would be idle to conceal that sometimes an incumbent and his parochial church council feel that the local authority ought to devote more labour or spend more money on a particular closed churchyard than they do, or, on the other hand, that a local authority sometimes feel that the incumbent and parochial church council are expecting too much and assuming that maintenance in decent order necessarily involves the same standard which they would adopt where a churchyard has been transferred for use as an open space under the Open Spaces Act 1906. Also sometimes a local authority take refuge in the fact that a neighbouring churchyard, whether closed or not, for which another parochial church council are responsible is in a worse state than the one about which complaint is made. But although many questions reach the Legal Advisory Commission about closed churchyards, it is significant that relatively few relate to serious disputes about the practical questions of maintenance and tribute should be paid to the understanding way in which most local authorities see that this task is carried out, especially as it is often difficult and unrewarding.

Appendix X

THE PASTORAL MEASURE 1968
A note on churchyards affected by redundancy

As has been noted in the chapter entitled Churchyards and the Law the land surrounding a consecrated church whether or not it is consecrated, and also detached consecrated burial grounds, are subject to the jurisdiction of the Bishop, exercised by the Diocesan Chancellor in the Consistory Court and in general no alterations may be made without the sanction of a faculty from the Court.

The Pastoral Measure 1968 contains powers which cut across this general provision. The Church Commissioners are empowered by Section 30 of the Measure to make pastoral schemes which may provide for the appropriation to such use or uses specified in the scheme of the whole or a part of a churchyard, or other land annexed or belonging to a church, or the whole or any part of any burial ground vested in the incumbent of a benefice which is not annexed to a church, and may also provide for the disposal of the land for these uses or without limitation of use. This power has been used to allow the erection of a parsonage house or parish hall within a churchyard. Where a churchyard affected by such a pastoral scheme has been used for burial and contains tombstones the provisions of Section 65 and Schedule 6 of the Measure for dealing with them, which are summarised later in this note, will apply.

The Commissioners have power under the Measure to make a pastoral scheme providing for a declaration of redundancy in respect of a consecrated church building. Such a scheme does not affect the churchyard and it remains vested in the incumbent and subject to faculty jurisdiction in the usual way although it may be affected by subsequent proceedings under the Measure.

When a church has been declared redundant, by a pastoral scheme, the Commissioners must within a period of three years from the date of redundancy prepare a further scheme, called a redundancy scheme, providing for the future of the building. The Measure provides three alternatives for the building's future, namely:

1. Appropriation to a suitable alternative use,
2. Vesting in the Redundant Churches Fund for care and maintenance, and
3. Demolition.

The Commissioners are empowered, when preparing a redundancy scheme (or a pastoral scheme under the special provisions of Sections 46 and 47 of the Measure), to include provisions dealing with the whole or a part of the churchyard annexed to the redundant church, whether or not it has been consecrated and used for burial. If the scheme provides for the appropriation of the building to a suitable alternative use, then it can further provide for the appropriation of the churchyard or a part of it to a use or uses specified in the scheme which would usually be ancillary to the use to which the building is to be put. The scheme may also provide for disposal of the church and churchyard by the Commissioners by sale gift or exchange or by the diocesan board of finance by lease. The power to make provision for the churchyard in a redundancy scheme (or a pastoral scheme under Section 46 or 47) is permissive and frequently only the building itself is appropriated to an alternative use leaving the churchyard or perhaps part of it unaffected, except that it is usually necessary to exercise the power given in the Measure to provide in the scheme for a right of way over the churchyard so as to give access to the redundant church to its new owner and allow for a right of access to that part of the churchyard surrounding the building for the purpose of carrying out repairs.

Where the scheme provides for the redundant church to be vested in the Redundant Churches Fund for care and maintenance it may also provide for the churchyard to vest in the Fund for a similar purpose. Usually the scheme so provides but there may well be circumstances (for example, the wish to continue to use the churchyard for burial) which make the vesting of it in the Fund appropriate. If so, a right of way for access and a right of access for repairs would be provided for in the scheme.

Where the scheme provides for the demolition of the redundant church it may also provide for the sale, lease, gift or exchange of the site of the building, with or without the whole or a part of the churchyard, either for a use specified in the scheme or without limitation of use. The scheme may also provide for the appropriation of the site of the building as an addition to the churchyard to remain vested in the incumbent.

The Commissioners must issue all pastoral and redundancy schemes as drafts and must consider any representations with respect to the scheme or any of their provisions before making the scheme and sending it for confirmation by Her Majesty in Council.

The Disused Burial Grounds Act 1884 prohibits the erection of buildings upon disused burial grounds. The Pastoral Measure 1968 removes this prohibition provided that no person has been buried there during the fifty years immediately prior to the coming into effect of a redundancy scheme or pastoral scheme which makes provisions for a churchyard or, if burials have taken place within fifty years, no relative or personal representative of the deceased person has objected to the scheme or if such objections have been made they have been withdrawn.

Where a redundancy or pastoral scheme provides for the disposal of a churchyard which has been used for burial it vests in either the Commissioners or the diocesan board of finance freed from burial rights. The Measure however makes provision for the payment of compensation for the loss of these rights.

Unless a redundancy scheme provides otherwise, a redundant church and churchyard affected by the scheme ceases to be subject to the legal effects of consecration and to Faculty Jurisdiction when the scheme becomes effective. The exception to this is where a redundant church, and perhaps the churchyard also, is vested in the Redundant Churches Fund. In this case the legal effects of consecration continue to apply, but Faculty Jurisdiction ceases.

Human Remains and Tombstones, Monuments and Memorials in churchyards affected by Schemes under the Measure

When a redundancy scheme or a pastoral scheme becomes effective which includes provision for the appropriation to other use of a churchyard or burial ground which has been used for burials and contains monuments of sepulture those provisions of the scheme which authorise its disposal for that use cannot be acted upon until the requirements of Section 65 of the Measure regarding the disposal of human remains and the disposal of tombstones required by Section 65 and carried out under the Schedule 6 procedure is not subject to representations although a notice must be published setting out the proposals for dealing with remains and tombstones and in some circumstances served upon next of kin or personal representatives of the deceased person and attention drawn to the right to undertake the removal of remains and the disposal of tombstones themselves in a manner other than that set out in the notice.

Section 65(1) of the Measure requires the person or body, usually the Church Commissioners or the Diocesan Board of Finance, in whom a redundant church and churchyard used for burials is vested by a redundancy scheme, to remove and re-inter or cremate all human remains and dispose of all tombstones monuments and memorials before demolishing, selling, leasing, or otherwise disposing of the property. But this provision does not apply to the Redundant Churches Fund cases; nor does it apply in the circumstances set out in section 65(2) of the Measure, *i.e.* where the redundant church is to be appropriated without structural change for use as a place of worship by a university, college, school, or other institution or by a church other than the Church of England. Moreover under section 65(3) of the Measure the Home Secretary may make an Order dispensing with this requirement so far as human remains are concerned in other cases if he is satisfied that the intended use or development of the property would not involve the disturbance of human remains. There is no provision in the Measure for a similar 'dispensing Order' in respect of the requirement of section 65(1) to dispose of tombstones, monuments and memorials commemorating deceased persons interred in the churchyard.

With regard to the disposal of monuments and memorials the Measure distinguishes between:

(a) those in commemorating deceased persons buried elsewhere than in the property affected by the redundancy scheme,

(b) and tombstones, monuments and memorials commemorating persons interred in the property which is the subject of the redundancy scheme.

Monuments and memorials under (a) are disposed of in such a manner as the Bishop, after consulting the Diocesan Advisory Committee, shall direct. Disposal in this way is often in practice taken to include a direction in suitable cases to leave them *in situ* in the church or churchyard although in cases where a church is to be demolished monuments from it must be disposed of by removal elsewhere or failing that by breaking up and defacing. Brass plates which have no intrinsic or historic interest may be buried after the inscriptions have been recorded and photographs taken.

As to tombstones, monuments or memorials under (b), the procedure for dealing with them is set out in Schedule 6 of the Measure. Where it is proposed to remove the human remains to which they relate and re-inter them elsewhere, the Measure contemplates where reasonably practicable the removal of the tombstones, monuments or memorials and setting them up in the new place of interment or other suitable place. (Where a tombstone is so worn that no inscription recording the name of the deceased survives, such procedure may be of little value and the procedure set out later under section 8 of Schedule 6 would normally be followed.)

If it is not proposed to remove the human remains because under section 65(3) of the Measure an Order has been made dispensing with this requirement, or if when the remains have been removed it has been found impracticable to transfer the tombstones to the new place of interment or other suitable place, then the procedure for disposal set out in section 8 of Schedule 6 is followed whereby the tombstones are offered by the landowner, generally the Commissioners or the Diocesan Board of

Finance, to the Bishop for preservation. He is required to consult the DAC about the disposal of a tombstone, monument or memorial and if, following this, they are not accepted by the Bishop for preservation the section requires the monument to be broken and defaced before being otherwise disposed of. Under this section the acceptance of a tombstone or other memorial by the Bishop for preservation and its subsequent disposal usually means in practice a direction that it should remain where it is if the use to which the church and churchyard is to be appropriated under the Scheme makes this course both practical and fitting.

In practice, therefore, it seems likely that tombstones from churchyards attached to redundant churches will only be defaced and broken up if

(a) no inscription remains, and then only if it is necessary to remove it from the churchyard to facilitate the use specified in the scheme, and

(b) where the specified use necessitates the removal of tombstones but not the human remains, and the DAC advises the Bishop that they are of no artistic or historic merit or interest.

If the tombstones remain *in situ*, the churchyard will pass into hands other than those of the church and there may be difficulties of access for the general public, unless the conveyance by the Church Commissioners, or the lease by the Diocesan Board of Finance make provision for such access. Where a grave is being tended regularly or some well-known person is buried, limited access is normally imposed in the conveyance or lease. Where the tombstones are not to remain *in situ*, but are of such merit that the Bishop accepts them for preservation, the difficulty is likely to be that of finding somewhere else to re-erect them, especially if the human remains are not also to be removed.

DIRECTORY OF ORGANISATIONS

Arboricultural Association, 59 Blythwood Gardens, Stansted, Essex (Tel. 027-971 3160)

Building Research Establishment (BRE), Building Research Station, Garston, Watford WD2 7JR (47-74040/76612)

Church Information Office (CIO), Church House, Dean's Yard, Westminster, London SW1P 3NZ (01-222 9011)

Civic Trust, 17 Carlton House Terrace, London SW1Y 5AW (01-930 0914)

Council for British Archaeology (CBA), 7 Marylebone Road, London NW1 (01-486 1527)

Council for Small Industries in Rural Areas (CoSIRA), Advisory Services Division, 35 Camp Road, Wimbledon Common, London SW19 4UP (01-946 5101)

Crafts Advisory Committee, 12 Waterloo Place, London SW1Y 4AU (01-839 8000)

Federation of Stone Industries, Alderman House, 37 Soho Square, London W1V 6AT (01-437 7107)

Joint Committee for the British Memorial Industry, Alderman House, 37 Soho Square, London W1V 6AT (01-437 7107)

Men of the Stones, The Rutlands, Trimwell, Stamford, Lincolnshire PE9 3UD (0780-3372)

National Association of Master Masons, Alderman House, Soho Square, London W1V 6AT (01-437 7107)

Society of Genealogists, 37 Harrington Gardens, London SW7 (01-373 7054)

Standing Joint Committee on Natural Stones, Alderman House, 37 Soho Square, London W1V 6AT (01-437 7107)

Standing Conference for Local History, 26 Bedford Square, London WC1B 3HU (01-636 4066)

Tree Council, Department of the Environment, Room C10/13, 2 Marsham Street, London SW1 (01-212 3876)

BIBLIOGRAPHY
(Especially recommended titles marked*)

Most of the undermentioned publications that are out of print are generally available through the regional and national inter-library lending system, for which readers are advised to contact their local public library.

NINETEENTH CENTURY TASTE

Armstrong, John	A paper on monuments 1848
Kelke, W. H.	The churchyard manual: intended chiefly for rural districts . . . with designs for churchyard memorials . . . finished by G. G. Scott . . . and W. Slater 1851
MacDonald, A. J.	Monuments, gravestones, burying grounds, cemeteries, temples etc 1848
Paget, Francis E.	A tract upon tombstones: or suggestions for the consideration of persons intending to set up that kind of monument to the memory of deceased friends 1843
Scott, George Gilbert	An appeal . . . against the Bill for the destruction of City churches and the sale of burial grounds 1854
Stone, Elizabeth	God's acre: or historical notices relating to the churchyard 1858
Trollope, Edward	Manual of sepulchral memorials 1858

LAW AND ADMINISTRATION

Church of England National Assembly	Pastoral Measure: no. 1, 1968 (repr. 1969) HMSO
*Elphinstone, Kenneth J. T.	A handbook of parish property. Mowbrays, 1973
Fellows, Alfred J.	The law of burial, and generally of the disposal of the dead. 2nd edition Hadden, Best and Co, 1952
Slade, F. V.	Church accounts, 2nd edition, Gee and Co, 1974

CARE AND MAINTENANCE

Council for the Care of Churches	Economical Churchyard Maintenance. CIO, 1970.
Fairbrother, Nan	New lives, new landscapes. Architectural Press, 1970; Penguin (paperback), 1973

Harvey, John	Conservation of old buildings. John Baker (A. & C. Black) 1972
Hopper, H. T.	Churchyard maintenance. (*In* the Church and School Handbook. 2nd edition Trade and Technical Press, 1974)
Hopper, H. T.	The provision and maintenance of playing fields and churchyards. Trade and Technical Press, 1967
*Insall, Donald	The care of old buildings today. Architectural Press, 1975

MONUMENTS AND EPITAPHS

Andrews, William	Curious epitaphs: collected from the graveyards of Great Britain and Ireland. Revised edition Hamilton, Adams, and Co, 1899
Batsford, Herbert and Godfrey, Walter H.	English mural monuments and tombstones. Batsford, 1916
Brown, Raymond Lamont	A book of epitaphs. David and Charles, 1969
*Burgess, Frederick	English churchyard memorials. Lutterworth, 1963
Church Commissioners	Pastoral Measure 1968: tombstones, monuments and memorials (UC8), Church Commissioners, 1973
Council for Places of Worship	A sheet of sample designs for memorials . . . Successor publication in course of preparation, to be entitled 'Pattern Book'. CIO
Day, E. Hermitage	Monuments and memorials. (The arts of the church), Mowbray, 1915
Jones, Jeremy	How to record a churchyard. Council for British Archaeology, due 1976
*Lindley, Kenneth	Graves and graveyards. (Local search series), Routledge, 1972
*Lindley, Kenneth	Of graves and epitaphs. Hutchinson, 1965
Munby, Arthur J.	Faithful servants: being epitaphs and obituaries recording their names and services. Reeves and Turner, 1891
National Association of Master Masons	The world's oldest craft: an appreciation of stonemasonry in the modern world. National Association of Master Masons, undated
Speight, Martin E.	Churchyard memorials: their recognition and recording. Standing Conference for Local History, due 1976
Tissington, Silvester	A collection of epitaphs and monumental inscriptions . . . Simpkin, Marshall and Co, 1857
Vincent, W. T.	In search of gravestones old and curious. Mitchell and Hughes, 1896
Weaver, Lawrence	Memorials and monuments old and new. Country Life, 1915

Whistler, Lawrence   Churchyard monuments in the 20th century. (Available from the Council for Places of Worship), 1973

White, H. Leslie   Elementary notes for churchyard recorders. (Revised edition obtainable from the Society of Genealogists), 1972

Whittick, Arnold   War memorials. Country Life, 1946

Wright, Geoffrey N.   Discovering epitaphs (Discovering series), Shire Publications, 1972

CROSSES AND LYCH-GATES

Messent, Claude J. W.   Lych-gates and their churches in eastern England: south Lincolnshire, Norfolk, Suffolk, north Essex, and east Cambridgeshire. The author, Blofields, Norwich, 1970

*Vallance, Aymer   Old crosses and lychgates. Batsford, 1920

SUNDIALS

Green, Arthur Robert   Sundials, incised dials or mass clocks. SPCK, 1926

Horne, Ethelbert   Primitive sundials or scratch dials. Barncott and Pearce, 1917

ARCHAEOLOGY

Council for Places of Worship Conservation Committee   Archaeology and churches. CPW 1974

Jesson, Margaret   The archaeology of churches: a report from the Churches Committee of the Council for British Archaeology . . . CBA, 1973

Rahtz, P. A.   The archaeology of the churchyard (*in* The Archaeological Study of Churches. CBA, due 1976)

STONEWORK

*Building and Research Establishment   Decay and conservation of stone masonry. (BRE Digest, 177), HMSO, 1975

Clarke, B. L. and Ashurst, J.   Stone preservation experiments. BRE, 1972

Schaffer, R. J.   The weathering of natural building stones, BRE, 1933 (reprinted 1972)

*Stone Industries   Natural stone directory. 3rd edition Stone Industries, 1974

FLORA AND FAUNA

*Barker, G. M. A.   Wildlife conservation in the care of churches and churchyards. CIO, 1972

Colvin, B. and Tyrwhitt, J.	Trees for town and country. 4th edition Lund Humphries, 1972
Cornish, Vaughan	The churchyard yew and immortality. Frederick Muller, 1946
*Department of the Environment	Notes on tree planting, maintenance and sources of information. HMSO, 1972
Hillier, Harold G.	Manual of trees and shrubs. David and Charles, 1972
James, N. D. G.	The arboriculturalist's companion. Basil Blackwell, 1972
Nicholson, B. E.	The Oxford book of trees. OUP, 1975
Pirone, P. P.	Tree maintenance. 4th edition Oxford University Press, 1972
*Pollard, Robert S. W.	Trees and the law. (Advisory booklet 6), Arboricultural Association, 1973

More comprehensive bibliographies on individual subjects are available on request from the Librarian of the Council for Places of Worship.